ENSLAVEMENT
and the
UNDERGROUND
RAILROAD
in
MISSOURI AND ILLINOIS

JULIE D. NICOLAI

THE
History
PRESS

Published by The History Press
Charleston, SC
www.historypress.com

Front cover, left: A slave dwelling, Valles Mines, Missouri. *Photograph by the author.*
Back cover: The Hood house, near Oakdale, Illinois. *Photograph by the author.*

First published 2023

Manufactured in the United States

ISBN 9781467154833

Library of Congress Control Number: 2023934842

This book is written in memory of all the brave souls who traveled along the Underground Railroad with the hope of finding freedom, individuality and rights reserved for all human beings, regardless of race, religion or gender.

St. Louis has been the crucible of American history…
the city at the heart of American history.
—*Walter Johnson,* The Broken Heart of America: St. Louis and the
Violent History of the United States

Tell me again we can lift the fingerprints of man from the blueprints of God.
—*Tanya Donelly,* "Salt" *(from the* Swan Song Series, *vol. 4)*

CONTENTS

ACKNOWLEDGEMENTS

I owe many sincere thanks to the following wonderful people for providing valuable information for this book: Sally Branson, Clare Casey (Ste. Genevieve National Historical Site), Amanda Clark (Missouri History Museum), Christopher Collins (Ste. Genevieve National Historical Site), Mazie Dalton, Angela da Silva, Ron "Johnny Rabbit" Elz, Hattie Felton (Missouri Historical Society), Dan Fuller (Bellefontaine Cemetery), Jim Goeken (Camp Warren Levis), Amy Haake (St. Charles County Historical Society), Andy Hahn (Campbell House Museum), Esley Hamilton, Nini Harris, Toi Hatcher (Missouri History Museum), Dea Hoover (Are We There Yet? Tours), Joan Huisinga, Dorris Keeven-Franke, Jeanne Keirle, Bill Kennedy, Mykel King (National Park Service intern), Jen Kirn (St. Mary of the Barrens Church), Linda Koenig, Angela Little (Collinsville Historical Museum), Mary-Christine McMahon (Glen Carbon Heritage Museum), Kathleen Schultz Mendez (Bethel Baptist Church, Caseyville), Corey Orr, Robbie Pratte (Center for French Colonial Life), John Reed (Holy Family Church), Eric Robinson, Nick Sacco (Ulysses S. Grant National Historic Site), Gina Seibe (Historic Florissant Inc.), William P. Shannon IV (St. Clair County Historical Society), Troy Taylor, Tandy Thomas (Center for French Colonial Life), Tom Thompson, Autumn Turkvant (National Park Service Intern), Sarah Umlauf and Brad Winn (Cahokia Courthouse State Historic Site). I am truly grateful to the many museum directors and personnel, archivists, librarians and National Park Service rangers—too numerous to mention here—who also contributed their insights and expertise to this book. I thank from the bottom of my heart all the longtime residents of Frontenac, Wildwood, Kirkwood, Webster Groves, Florissant, Ferguson, Bridgeton, Alton, et cetera, who provided me with oral interviews on many of the sites in this book. They also passed on the long oral traditions of their ancestors concerning these sites. Finally, thanks to my family, friends and pets, who have inspired and supported me unconditionally from the beginning.

INTRODUCTION

Prophecy is only brilliant memory.
—*Marilyn Robinson,* Housekeeping

The Underground Railroad system, a pathway to liberty for freedom seekers (enslaved people fleeing their enslavers), is a subject to be approached with an open mind and bountiful heart. This chapter in American history is fraught with danger, hardship, sorrow and joy. It is populated by a diverse group, some heroic and some villainous—courageous freedom seekers, fearless free Black and white Underground Railroad conductors and agents, pro- and antislavery politicians, ardent abolitionists and heartless traders and hunters of the enslaved.

The Underground Railroad has been described by the National Park Service as "the exacting conscience of the most important reform movement in U.S. history—purging the land of slavery," and "one of history's finest symbols of the struggle against oppression."*

The Underground Railroad, arguably one of the most effective resistance movements in world history, is an integral part of both Black American history and United States history. We must not forget or deny it, or the horror will start all over again. The Underground Railroad system offered a treacherous but hopeful journey to the freeing of not only the physical body but the indomitable spirit.

---

* *Underground Railroad: Official National Park Handbook.*

NOTE TO READER: In this book, I will refer to enslaved people fleeing their enslavers as "freedom seekers." The terms "fugitive slave," "runaway slave" and "escaped slave" were mainly used by white people and imply that these freedom seekers were doing something wrong. While, technically, what they were doing was illegal, it was done to overcome an unfair, cruel, oppressive, hateful, unethical and immoral white man's law. Freedom seekers chose to pursue a course to liberty that every human being is entitled to under the laws of the powers that be. Spiritual, emotional, physical and intellectual freedom are not given or taken away by the law of any human being.

Specific addresses are not listed, as the majority of these sites are on private property and closed to the public. The addresses for many of the sites that are on public land or open to the public can be found on the internet. The individual sites are listed in only rough geographical order. Therefore, it may be helpful for the reader to have maps of Missouri and Illinois handy for reference.

PART I

THE UNDERGROUND RAILROAD IN MISSOURI AND ILLINOIS

When I remember that with the waters of her [the United States'] *noblest rivers, the tears of my brethren are borne to the ocean, disregarded and forgotten, and that her most fertile fields drink daily of the warm blood of my outraged sisters, I am filled with unutterable loathing.*

—Frederick Douglass

1

OVERVIEW

The Underground Railroad was not a real railroad at all; rather, it was a system of paths, waterways and tracks used by freedom seekers to escape their bondage and find freedom, usually in the northern United States or Canada, although some fled to the Caribbean, Mexico or the western United States. It used code words borrowed from the real railroads. "Stations" were safe houses where freedom seekers were hidden, "conductors" organized transfers and routes, "cargo" referred to the freedom seekers, "agents" transferred the cargo. The "North Star" referred to the direction to follow and the "promised land" was Canada. Quilts may have been used to provide signals. Brick patterns in chimneys, topsy-turvy dolls and lights from cupolas were also used to signal whether the coast was clear.

It is thought that some Black spirituals contained codes that were used by freedom seekers. Although first published in the early twentieth century, songs like "Wade in the Water" and "Follow the Drinking Gourd" date back to at least the first half of the nineteenth century. We are not sure who wrote them or exactly when they were written. The drinking gourd was code for the Big Dipper, which pointed to the North Star and guided freedom seekers in the right direction. The famous Underground Railroad conductor Harriet Tubman used "Wade in the Water" to tell freedom seekers to go through water to hide their scent from the dogs of hunters of enslaved people. It is also a "map song," in which directions were coded into the lyrics. Songs such as these were used on the Underground Railroad to give directions, provide instructions or simply instill hope and strength in the freedom seeker. Other examples include "Steal Away" and "Swing Low, Sweet Chariot."

Black and white, men and women, were involved in the Underground Railroad. The wives of conductors provided food and clothing for the freedom seekers, and many were actively involved in the moving and sheltering of them (see, for example, the story of Archer Alexander later in this book). Free Black people played an integral role in the Underground Railroad system.

This Underground Railroad system was covert, and therefore, activists of the time, for the most part, did not keep written records regarding it. There were a few documented Underground Railroad stations. We learn most of what we know about the Underground Railroad from primary newspaper articles, court records, correspondence, diaries, memoirs, advertisements in newspapers offering rewards for freedom seekers and narratives of conductors and freedom seekers. We also rely on long oral histories and traditions extending well into the nineteenth century that were handed down through generations to learn about specific sites.

BEGINNINGS

The lucrative triangular trade included the business of forcibly transporting Africans to the new world to be traded for money or goods or bought with cash to work on plantations and farms in areas that practiced slavery. The infamous route of the slavers and their ships went from Europe to West Africa and then the Caribbean and the Americas before going back to Europe. The portion of the route between Africa and the Americas was known as the Middle Passage. On this long, treacherous voyage, the suffering of the enslaved was beyond comprehension, and some even jumped overboard to escape a future life of bondage, abuse and separation from family.

According to the Trans-Atlantic Slave Trade Database, 12.5 million Africans were kidnapped and put on ships to the Americas between 1501 and 1866. Of them, 1 million died from disease, starvation and other causes. There were forty thousand of these trips across the Atlantic that lasted on average for sixty days. Examples of the horrific conditions on the slave ships could be seen on the *Sao Jose-Paquete de Africa*, which wrecked off the coast of Cape Town, South Africa, in 1794. Its suffering human cargo consisted of five hundred Africans who were captured in Mozambique. They were shackled and crammed like sardines inside the 130-foot-long ship, lying in their own filth. The *Clotilda* was the last known ship to bring enslaved people from Africa to America. It arrived illegally in Mobile, Alabama, in 1860.

Although the importation of enslaved people to the United States was abolished in 1808, that did little to abet the use of enslaved people as forced laborers in the South. By 1860, there were almost four million enslaved people in this country. One might wonder how they got here. Some arrived via the illegal slave trade that was active in coastal regions, some were the result of intermarriage among the enslaved and some were the product of the systematic and endemic raping of enslaved people by their enslavers. White enslavers raped enslaved women at will. Their white sons raped enslaved women as a rite of passage into manhood. Enslaved men were forced to rape enslaved women, thus becoming rape victims themselves. Abolitionist firebrand Elijah Lovejoy said, "More than half of those critical of abolitionism had several relations with slave women." This is an undeniable part of our nation's history, but it is one of the most difficult for us to talk about. It is time we acknowledge it, take responsibility for it and give reparations to the descendants of these enslaved people.

SLAVERY IN THE ST. LOUIS REGION

Early Jesuits in the area were enslavers (initially circa 1699 at a Jesuit settlement on the River Des Peres, south of downtown St. Louis in the Carondelet area). In the Revolutionary War's Battle of Fort San Carlos (1780), enslaved people helped successfully defend St. Louis (under Spanish rule) against the British and their Native allies, thus preventing the opening of the Mississippi Valley to the British. The French in St. Louis enslaved African and Native people, who were governed by the Code Noir (or Black Code), which gave them limited rights but certainly more than what the later Anglo version of slavery provided them. With the 1803 Louisiana Purchase, the area became a territory of the United States, and white settlers moved in, bringing with them their version of the "peculiar institution," one of brutality and oppression. The Fugitive Slave Acts (1793 and 1850) allowed for the capture and return of fugitives within United States territory.

In a nutshell, the Missouri Compromise of 1820 ultimately brought Missouri into the Union as a slave state (1821) and Maine as a free state. In general, slavery in Missouri was carried out on a smaller scale than it was in the Southern states. Most of the large farms were concentrated along the Missouri River in the central part of the state in an area called Little Dixie. There were also plantations and farms in the Missouri Bootheel, St. Louis City and St. Louis County and in the western portion of the state. William Wells Brown, a famous abolitionist, was enslaved as a youth in St. Louis. We might assume slavery in the South was harsher than slavery in Missouri, but Wells, while attempting to escape, was treed by dogs and severely whipped. His narrative recounts brutal masters and violent abuse of the enslaved in the St. Louis area.

The 1847 records of the St. Louis coroner reveal the appalling murder of an enslaved child: "Eight-year-old Sarah, the property of Leona Cordell, was evidently whipped to death….Of all the inquests that I have held, numbering thirty-seven, and having seen as I thought the work of death in almost all its horrors, the above case far surpasses anything I have ever seen of human depravity and cruelty."

In 1834, a U.S. Army officer in St. Louis whipped an enslaved girl to death. The venue for his trial was changed to St. Charles, and he was found not guilty.

William Wells Brown related that William Greenleaf Eliot, a Unitarian minister who founded Washington University in 1853, saw a neighbor's enslaved woman hanging by her thumbs and being flogged by her enslaver. Wells witnessed an enslaved woman crawling around her enslaver's St. Louis property, dragging manacles behind her. He also saw enslaved people taken into the streets of St. Louis by their enslavers and publicly beaten.

Wells once said, "St. Louis slave owners were the most barbarous of those anywhere." He reported that slave trader William Walker raped one of his enslaved women multiple times. He had four children with her and then sold her "down the river." Wells went on to indicate that an enslaved man, Aaron, was beaten so badly by a Mr. Colburn with a cowhide whip, he had to be washed down with rum. Mary Armstrong, born enslaved in St. Louis circa 1845, described her enslaver as follows: "Old satan in torment couldn't be no meaner than [he] was to the slaves." Gaius Paddock, as quoted in the Missouri History Museum's *Mighty Mississippi* exhibit, indicated the Old Courthouse had a whipping post on one corner and a slave pen on the other.

St. Louis had over twenty slave dealers at one time, the most prominent being the infamous Bernard Lynch. He owned a slave market at 100 Locust Street. In 1859, he bought a larger building, which served as a slave pen, at Fifth and Myrtle Streets (now Broadway and Clark Avenue). This structure had barred windows and locks, effectively turning it into a prison. According to a firsthand account, the enslaved people were kept in a room with a dirt floor, three benches and only one small window. The building (Myrtle Street Prison), demolished in the twentieth century, was used by the Union as a prison during the Civil War. The Meyer Brothers Drug Store was later built over the pens. A National Park Service ranger at the Jefferson National Expansion Memorial indicated that the basement of the pen, with chains in the walls, was discovered during construction excavations near Busch Stadium. Lynch placed a chillingly suggestive advertisement in a local newspaper, indicating "particular attention was paid to the selecting of homes for favorite servants."

Another documented slave trader was Corbin and Thompson, who had a slave market at 3 South Sixth Street, between Pine and Chestnut Streets. Bolton, Diggins and Co. was a slave-trading firm in the area around the present-day arch. Enslavers from Arkansas, New Orleans, Natchez, et cetera, came to the St. Louis slave markets to buy enslaved people. An advertisement for an 1843 sheriff's sale of enslaved people at the Old Courthouse indicated seventeen enslaved people under the age of thirty were to be sold.

On the other hand, some St. Louis residents, outraged by the horrors of slavery, took it upon themselves to advocate for its abolition. For example, Frances Dana Gauge, who moved to the city in 1853, was so ardent in her antislavery stance that the *Missouri Republican* newspaper refused to publish her articles, and her house was burned more than once. In 1863, the American Freedom School was established by James Yeatman and William Greenleaf Eliot to educate freed Black people and freedom seekers. Located in the Ebenezer Church on Washington Avenue, it was burned down two days after it was created but soon relocated to a new spot.

Sharlaine Landwehr tells of the St. Louis Button Works building, which was built in the mid-nineteenth century. Her ancestor W.C. Ayer owned the St. Louis Button Works, established in 1893. He reported that the basement of the building had a ten-by-thirty-foot room with shackles attached to one of the walls. Before it became the St. Louis Button Works, enslaved people were chained there, possibly as punishment or while they were waiting to be sold. Ayer took new employees to the basement to see the shackles and impress upon them how wrong slavery was.

A freedom suit was a lawsuit filed by an enslaved person, who may have been represented by an attorney, petitioning a court for freedom. In Missouri, they stemmed from an 1807 territorial statute allowing a person held in wrongful servitude to sue for freedom. In addition, an 1824 Missouri law stated, "once free, always free." Today, the freedom suits leave us with an important record of the names and situations of some of

This photograph of Lynch's Slave Pen was taken by famous St. Louis photographer Thomas Easterly and shows the exterior of the pen. Bernard Lynch is one of the men shown, but we do not know which one. Lynch's Slave Market, *Thomas Easterly, photograph, circa 1852, Missouri Historical Society, identifier N17134, https://collections. mohistory.org/resource/142174.*

the enslaved people in the area. Between 1807 and 1857, over 280 freedom suits were filed in the St. Louis Circuit Court; 110 were successful. Some of the more well-known St. Louis freedom suits include those of Dred Scott (see section later in this book), Polly Wash (1839) and Lucy Delaney (1842). Wash and Delaney eventually won their freedom. Ground was broken for the Freedom Suits Memorial at the Civil Courts Building in downtown St. Louis in 2021.

In 1860, 2 percent of the total population of St. Louis County was composed of enslaved people, but it had the seventh-largest population of enslaved people in the state of Missouri.[†]

Probate auctions, which included the sale of enslaved people, then considered merely property, were held at the first two log churches on the grounds of the current Old Cathedral and then at the Old Courthouse. The slave dealers held auctions of enslaved persons, at times exhibiting them naked to prospective buyers, thus establishing dominance over and humiliating the oppressed. There was a profitable business of enslavers from Kentucky, Tennessee, Maryland and Delaware selling enslaved people in St. Louis to be taken down the Mississippi River to the Deep South. Auctions of the enslaved were also held at the St. Charles County Courthouse (now demolished) on South Main Street in St. Charles starting around 1840. The notice for one of the last public auctions of enslaved people in St. Louis appeared in the *Missouri Republican* on December 28, 1860. Seven enslaved men from a local estate were to be sold on New Year's Day. Jim was auctioned off, but the sale of the other six men was postponed until May.

---

† Mutti Burke, *On Slavery's Border*.

Slave holding cells underneath Lynch's Slave Pen. Former Slave Pen, *St. Louis Post-Dispatch, May 15, 2014.*

The Anti-Abolition Society was formed by wealthy St. Louis enslavers at a meeting at the Old Courthouse in 1846. Its members included McKelvey, Dorsett, Bissel, Price, Skinker and Sappington. Frederick Dent, U.S. Grant's father-in-law, served as treasurer. They traveled to Jefferson City to lobby for the 1846 laws restricting enslaved people, which were passed.

Slave patrols were established by the Missouri legislature in 1825. From Missouri, the patrols and other "hunters" often crossed into Illinois to track their quarry. It was a lucrative business to sell captured freedom seekers "down the river" or send them back to their owners. One hunter of enslaved persons purportedly lived at 3316 Lemp in St. Louis City. During the Civil War (1861–65), some freedom seekers fled to Union contraband camps. The men might have run away to join the United States Colored Troops, as was the probable case of Elijah Madison, who was enslaved on the Coleman plantation in the Wildwood area, west of St. Louis County. He ended up at Benton Barracks, now the site of Fairgrounds Park in St. Louis, but we are not sure how he got there.

In her book on freedom seekers in Missouri, Harriet Frazier includes a chart of people who were imprisoned in Missouri for assisting freedom seekers from 1839 to 1865.‡ Nine people were convicted in St. Louis County between 1840 and 1861. The *St. Louis Globe-Democrat*, on July 16, 1856, reported, "Underground Railroad agents…are said to have assisted [freedom seekers]."

ROUTES

Although most people associate the Underground Railroad with areas east of Illinois, that state played an integral role in helping freedom seekers. In 1860, Missouri had approximately 115,000 enslaved people, composing around 10 percent of the state's population. St. Louis, although located in a slave state, was certainly involved in the effort of the Underground Railroad, likely even having a network of affiliates that assisted freedom seekers throughout the St. Louis region. This makes sense for several reasons. St. Louis is situated on the Mississippi River, the major north–south artery from New Orleans to Minneapolis, a perfect escape route. The Little Dixie area, where the enslaved were concentrated in Missouri, starts west of St. Louis and stretches across the state. One straightforward escape route was to get to St. Louis, cross the river and use the many routes through Illinois to Canada. Freedom seekers could go to the Halls Ferry area of north St. Louis County and cross the river via Portage des Sioux to Alton, Illinois, a major Underground Railroad hub. They could also cross the Mississippi River at St. Louis and head to Brooklyn, a free Black community founded by Priscilla "Mother" Baltimore; one of the other free Black communities; or an Underground Railroad town with safe houses. Underground Railroad maps of Illinois are crisscrossed with a plethora of routes. St. Louis had farms with enslaved people, a large German abolitionist population, French remnants and about 1,500 free Black people—the perfect storm for the Underground Railroad. Before the Civil War, there were around 2,000 enslaved people in St. Charles County, adjacent to St. Louis County. Dan's Ferry at Carondelet (originally an independent city, it became part of St. Louis City in the 1870s) was a crossing point for freedom seekers moving from Missouri to Illinois.

‡ Frazier, *Runaway & Freed Missouri Slaves.*

Those involved in the Underground Railroad in the St. Louis area included Priscilla Baltimore, the Robersons, Artemis Bullard at the Rock house (in Webster Groves, St. Louis County), Nathaniel Hanson (Alton, Illinois), John Berry and Mary Meachum, Isaac Kelly (Alton, Illinois), Peter and Nancy Ann Hudlin (St. Louis City), William Greenleaf and Margaret Eliot and Elijah Lovejoy. Bellefontaine Cemetery, one of the most important historic garden cemeteries in the country, founded in 1849, holds the graves of the Robersons; Priscilla Baltimore; Artemis Bullard, the enslaver of Caroline Quarlls; Nelly Warren (enslaved by the Collier family); John Anderson; and the Meachums (although Mary's inscription is a cenotaph).

Examples of Local Freedom Seekers
Who Used the Underground Railroad

Caroline Quarlls (1826–1892) was born into slavery in St. Louis. Her parents were her white enslaver, Robert Pryor Quarlls, and her enslaved mother ("Quarlls" is the spelling most used by her family). She escaped to Sandwich, Canada, via Alton, Illinois; Milwaukee; and Detroit in 1842. Her Underground Railroad conductor in Wisconsin was Lymon Goodnow, who wrote an account of her escape in *The History of Waukesha County, Wisconsin*. This is a rare example of an extant firsthand account of a journey along the Underground Railroad. Goodnow compassionately described her as follows: "She was probably an octaroon…with a straight nose, thin lips, skin not very dark and slender form of medium height. Although quite intelligent, she could not read or write….She was occasionally whipped while in bondage…[and was a] house slave….She did fine sewing, embroidery and waited on her mistress." Caroline later married a former enslaved man in Canada, and they had six children.

Archer Alexander (circa 1810–1880) was born into slavery in Virginia. According to local historian, author, lecturer and Alexander expert Dorris Keeven Franke, Alexander's enslaver brought him to St. Charles County (adjacent to St. Louis County). During the Civil War, he fled after alerting Union troops at the blockhouse at Peruque Creek that the bridge was going to be sabotaged by Confederates. Alexander ended up in St. Louis City, where he was assisted by William Greenleaf and Margaret Eliot. William wrote *The Story of Archer Alexander* in 1885. Alexander went on to become the model for the Black man breaking his chains on the Emancipation Memorial (1876) in Washington, D.C.

Frederick Sams was enslaved at Franklinville, Daniel Bissell's estate. According to the *Missouri Gazette* on February 15, 1817, Bissell believed Sams had fled to Florissant or St. Louis City and offered a twenty-five-dollar reward for his capture. The article also stated that Sams "had some marks of the whip on his back."

Several other related local events should certainly be mentioned. Of course, the Dred and Harriet Scott freedom suit, partially tried at the Old Courthouse in St. Louis, was a major impetus for the Civil War. Supreme Court chief justice Roger Taney wrote the majority opinion, ruling that all Black people—enslaved as well as free—were not and could never become citizens of the United States and, therefore, had no right to sue in federal court.

A portrait of Caroline Quarlls. *Wisconsin Historical Society,* WHS-52619.

In 1836, the brutal burning in St. Louis of biracial boatman Francis McIntosh at the hands of a mob without a trial or due process horrified the nation. McIntosh was arrested in conjunction with a skirmish. McInstosh asked his arresting officers how long he would be jailed. One told him he could be jailed for five years, which frightened McIntosh, who then stabbed one officer to death and injured another. A white mob broke into his cell and took him to a tree, where he was lynched. The event provoked the ardent abolitionist Elijah Lovejoy to write of McIntosh's scorched face screaming to be shot. McIntosh burned for eighteen minutes before he finally perished. Two years later, Abraham Lincoln commented on the lynching, which he labeled "revolting to humanity." He continued, "His story is very short and is, perhaps, the most highly tragic of anything of its length that has ever been witnessed in real life. A mulatto man by name of McIntosh was seized in the street, dragged to the suburbs of the city, chained to a tree and actually burned to death; and all within a single hour from the time he had been a freeman." A grand jury, headed by the appropriately named Judge Luke E. Lawless, convened, but no one was ever charged or convicted for the murder.

From 1850 to 1855, Celia, a fourteen-year-old enslaved girl, was raped and abused by her enslaver, Robert Newsom, a Callaway County, Missouri farmer. At least one child was born of the forced liaisons. In 1855, the courageous Celia had enough and gave Newsom what he deserved: a deadly

A detail of an illustration of the burning of Francis McIntosh. Burning of McIntosh at St. Louis, in April 1836, *in* Illustrations of the American Anti-Slavery Almanac for 1840 *(New York: American Anti-Slavery Society, 1840).*

beating with a stick. Although her attorneys argued the killing was done in self-defense, unsurprisingly, the jury found her guilty, and she was hanged while pregnant with Newsom's child.

Even after the Civil War, John Buckner was accused of attempting to rape a white woman and of raping a Black woman. He was ultimately lynched from a railroad bridge by a mob without a trial or due process in Valley Park, St. Louis County, Missouri. No one was ever punished for the lynching.

Barbara Woods, the director emeritus of the African American Studies Department at St. Louis University, indicated, "What we do know through some research is Underground Railroad activity certainly was taking place in Missouri. We know there was activity in St. Louis just because of our neighbor Illinois. In terms of getting the documentation, it's not there. The leads are very interesting and very exciting."

2

MISSOURI UNDERGROUND RAILROAD SITES

850 Rochedale Drive, Kirkwood, St. Louis County (Circa 1850, Demolished)

The Underground Railroad ran through Kirkwood and Webster Groves along the routes of the real railroad. This house was a two-story farmhouse. During remodeling, a tunnel was discovered in the basement leading to nearby Dougherty Ferry Road. Unfortunately, this house was demolished in 2014.

Seven Gables (Judge Enos Clarke House), Kirkwood, St. Louis County, Missouri (1913)

This house replaced his earlier home Woodlawn (mid-1860s). It was on a lot that was associated with the Underground Railroad. Woodlawn burned around 1904. Clark was a Radical Republican and went to Washington, D.C., in 1863 with others to see Lincoln at a meeting regarding federal government policy in Missouri.

The house on Rochedale Drive. *Photograph by the author.*

1015 SPOEDE ROAD, FRONTENAC, ST. LOUIS COUNTY (1830S, DEMOLISHED)

There are conflicting long oral traditions surrounding this house. One says it was an Underground Railroad station. The other says enslaved people were auctioned off on the property. It is possible, considering it was built around thirty years before the end of the Civil War, that it served both purposes under separate owners. This house's architecture was reminiscent of that of the Bolduc house in Ste. Genevieve, Missouri, and the Menard house in Kaskaskia, Illinois. It originally may have had a gallery around three or four sides. Much of the information in this section comes from Elinor Martineau Coyle's book *Old St. Louis Homes, 1764–1865, the Stories They Tell* (1979). She received her information from an elderly Black woman whose parents were enslaved who was living in a Black section of Richmond Heights, which had its beginnings on land that was given to freed enslaved people by their enslavers. Ms. Coyle had a reputation for being a very thorough researcher. The building's St. Louis County historic inventory sheet indicates the porch was added later.

Snyder House, Frontenac, St. Louis County (1854)

Eleanor Martineau Coyle, an iconic local author of books on St. Louis architecture, examined the house and found a hiding place within the basement wall. I talked to the owner of the house in 2021, and she said she had not found any evidence of a hiding place in the house and that it was not involved in Underground Railroad activities. It is possible that at some point, the hiding place was bricked over and is now hard to delineate. According to the home's current owner, the house was built around 1854 by the Snyders' enslaved people, some of the same people who built Old Des Peres Presbyterian Church. Snyder was an early settler of the area and owned land around Old Des Peres Presbyterian Church and Mercy Retreat Center. Snyder was buried in the Old Des Peres Presbyterian Church Cemetery, and his marker is in relatively good condition.

The Snyder house. *Photograph by the author.*

OLD DES PERES PRESBYTERIAN CHURCH, FRONTENAC, ST. LOUIS COUNTY (CIRCA 1833)

This historic rock church was built by local enslaved people around 1833. Enslavers Hartshorn, Maddox and Small contributed one acre of land each for the site of the church. Stephen Maddox enslaved at least twelve people, a large number for the area. The original landowners stipulated that the congregation set aside part of the land for a cemetery, with a designated section for the burials of the enslaved. The church was located in a pro-Southern farming area that had been settled by people from Virginia and Kentucky. French settlers and abolitionist Germans also lived in the area. Around 1838, it was used as a meetinghouse for the German Evangelical Zion Church, which began keeping records in 1838. They buried some members in the cemetery before moving to their own church in 1839 (now Parkway United Church of Christ).

The famous abolitionist martyr Elijah Lovejoy was certified as a minister at this church in March 1834 (documented in extant primary Presbytery records and confirmed by Esley Hamilton in his book on St. Louis County architecture). He was also in St. Charles and Alton, where he was murdered in 1837 while defending his printing press from a proslavery mob. In 1827, Lovejoy moved to St. Louis, where he taught school and wrote for a Whig journal, the *Times*, and the *Missouri Republican*. He left St. Louis to attend Princeton Theological Seminary and later converted to Presbyterianism. In 1832, Lovejoy returned to St. Louis and started the *St. Louis Observer*, a religious newspaper with an antislavery bent.

A former pastor of the church, Robert Tabscott, purportedly had copies of three letters signed by Lovejoy. One addressed to the Home Missionary Society described Lovejoy's work at Old Des Peres.

Inside the church, there was a room under the floorboards where freedom seekers were hidden. A trapdoor in the floor provided access to it. I grew up across the street from the church, and in the 1970s, my father and I would walk over and talk to the conservation architects who were renovating the church. They had thoroughly researched the site and showed us the room under the floor. I was even allowed to be lifted down into the room to see what it would have been like for the brave freedom seekers who hid there. The room's method of construction, age, size and materials used to build it are comparable to that of other Underground Railroad hiding places I have seen. The hidden room was extremely old and probably original to the church. It would not have been used for storage, as it was too small and

Old Des Peres Presbyterian Church. *Photograph by the author.*

there were likely outbuildings for that purpose. The only thing it could have been was a hiding place. The mother church, Faith Des Peres Presbyterian Church, notes on its website that "the church was rumored to be a well-known stop along the Underground Railroad." It is most likely that it was used on the Underground Railroad during the tenure of the German Evangelical Zion Church (late 1830s). Unfortunately, the hiding place was destroyed when a crawl space was added during or after renovations. The conservation architects also found a tunnel entrance but did not excavate it to see where it went. This church may have worked in cooperation with the nearby Snyder farm (see its previous section) on the Underground Railroad. In his book *Discovering African American St. Louis: A Guide to Historic Sites*, John A. Wright says that it "was used as a station on the Underground Railroad."

Old Des Peres Presbyterian Church. *Photograph by the author.*

According to the *Missouri Republican* on July 6, 1863, Johanna, an enslaved girl of Turner Maddox, Stephen's son, drowned at the age of seventeen in his cistern. The verdict of the jury was that she died by suicide. She might have been buried in the Maddox family plot with other enslaved people or in the unmarked section for enslaved people in the southeast corner of the cemetery.

Enslaved people and soldiers from the Civil War, among others, were buried in the cemetery (see part II). Northern supporters and Southern sympathizers sat in pews together during the Civil War. Yankee soldiers named the church the "Old Stone Meeting House." Information on the burial sites of enslaved people can be found in chapter 6 of this book.

Rock House (now Great Circle), Webster Groves, St. Louis County (Circa 1850)

This house was built by Artemis Bullard, an ardent abolitionist, Underground Railroad conductor and relative of Harriet Beecher Stowe, who wrote the famous *Uncle Tom's Cabin*. From 1850 to 1855, it was Webster College, a seminary for young men, and purportedly a front for Underground Railroad activity. Sadly, Bullard was killed in a train accident on the Gasconade River Bridge in 1855. He was buried in Bellefontaine Cemetery in St. Louis County. The Rock House also served as a Western Sanitary Commission hospital during the Civil War and a home for refugees, both Black and white.

A tunnel, several blocks long, led from the Rock House to a large home on the other side of the hill, which still has the sealed-off tunnel entrance in the basement. The tunnel entrance at the Rock House was sealed in the 1890s, when, legend has it, two children got lost and died in the tunnel. There was also a secret room in the house. Today, there is no longer any evidence of this room left. In the late 1980s, during a repaving of the parking lot west of the Rock House, a tunnel entrance with steps was found. Unfortunately, it was paved over, but an original beam and stone are on display inside the house.

The Underground Railroad was active in Webster Groves, although there were also farms with enslaved people in the area. James Marshall was an enslaver but eventually freed them and gave them land on Euclid, north of the Rock House. Descendants of these people still live in the area. Marshall gave or sold the land for the Rock House to Bullard.

Some of this information was gathered from an interview with Susan Corrington, the former director of development, historian and archivist for Edgewood Children's Home (now Great Circle).

Helfenstein Mansion, Webster Groves, St. Louis County (1857)

This house was designed by architect Robert Mitchell, who helped design the Old Courthouse downtown. During the Civil War, Helfenstein was a Northern sympathizer. General U.S. Grant was a friend of Helfenstein and visited him at the house frequently. According to Marilyn Bradley in *City of Century*

Homes: A Centennial History of Webster Groves, Missouri, "There are claims that the basement was used as a station for the Underground Railroad. Tunnels led from the basement to Shady Creek, along Kirkham Road."

TAVERN ON VAN HORN FARM (NOW MT. CAVALRY LUTHERAN CHURCH), BRENTWOOD, ST. LOUIS COUNTY (TAVERN, DEMOLISHED)

This is the site of a rock tavern on the Van Horns' farm. It served as an Underground Railroad safe house and was later a school and then a church.

DEHODIAMONT HOUSE, ST. LOUIS CITY (CIRCA 1829)

A 2002 *St. Louis Post-Dispatch* article indicated there is "a secret room with a secret compartment in it" in this house. It was heavily altered in 1871. In August 2020, I talked to a man in his seventies who lives next door to this house. He told me he went in the home when he was eight years old and was told its history by his family at that time. He saw tunnels in the basement, but he did not go through them to find out where they went. They had stone and brick walls (like the coal chute in the Hanson house, see the

The DeHodiamont house.
Photograph by the author.

next section). He indicated that now, a cast iron trapdoor covers the tunnel entrance in the basement. The tunnels are still there and were used on the Underground Railroad. He also noted the house had a chimney on either side and a hidden bedroom upstairs. DeHodiamont held slave auctions in the backyard. He used a podium and put the sale book on it. Later on, it became an Underground Railroad station.

HALLS FERRY AREA, JUNCTION OF NEW HALLS FERRY AND DOUGLAS, FLORISSANT, ST. LOUIS COUNTY

Hall was a friend of Elijah Lovejoy and hid freedom seekers in the limestone bluffs near Halls Ferry. He owned a ferry that he used to take freedom seekers across the Missouri River to Portage des Sioux and then across the Mississippi River to Alton, Illinois.

Florissant was a pro-Southern area and had farms with enslaved people until Germans later moved in. Nearby Hazelwood was part of a network of farms along the Missouri River in Florissant Valley. It was home to Confederate general Daniel Frost and his wife, Lily, during the Civil War era.

According to Gina Seibe of Historic Florissant Inc., there is an oral tradition that says the farms in the Jamestown area had tunnels leading to the river that were part of the Underground Railroad.

3170 FEE FEE ROAD, BRIDGETON, ST. LOUIS COUNTY (CIRCA 1790–1820, THE 1840S AND THE 1920S, DEMOLISHED, EXCEPT FOR CABIN, WHICH IS IN STORAGE)

The oldest section of this house was built between 1790 and 1820. Later sections were built in the 1840s and 1920s. It was an Underground Railroad safe house with a hidden room in the basement and a tunnel leading to the creek that runs through the park behind the house. The oldest portion of the house was a log structure with gun ports in its walls. The library (part of the 1840s section of the home) was built around it. A rear addition was constructed in the 1920s.

This house was up for sale in 2018 for $350,000. Ultimately, a developer ended up buying it and tearing it down to make way for a subdivision. When the house was for sale, I took a tour and was able to examine its basement. There was definitely a hidden space in the front wall of the room in the northwest corner of the basement. One of the owners wanted to excavate it but never got around to it. This owner said in an old newspaper article that he had some college students go into the tunnel, but they were never able to get to its other end. There was a fireplace that ran all the way from the basement to the second floor. The fireplace protruded prominently into the living space from the wall's façade (versus protruding from the exterior of the house), as if there was a hiding place inside. (It looked similar to the hiding spot in the fireplace of Dr. David Nelson's house, an Underground Railroad safe house discussed later in this book.) It is probable this was a false fireplace with a hiding place inside.

There was a well in the backyard protected by a well house. There was also a second "well" behind the house that was uncapped (just a hole in the ground covered by boards). There were also holes in the ground surrounded by concrete along the east side of the house, which revealed a flooded underground area. I was able to look inside them and the well. The entire area, including the space along the entire east wall of the house, was filled with water. This certainly could have been a tunnel at one time, with the

3170 Fee Fee Road. *Photograph by the author.*

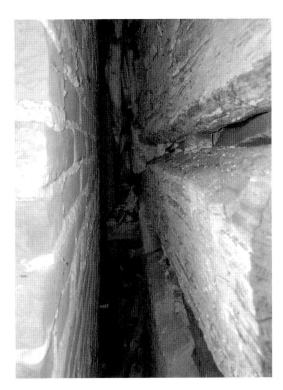

Left: The wooden walls of "McKay's Fort," later embedded within brick walls, 3170 Fee Fee Road. *Photograph by the author.*

Below: A basement room with a fireplace and a protruding section of the lower wall, 3170 Fee Fee Road. *Photograph by the author.*

The main floor fireplace, 3170 Fee Fee Road. *Photograph by the author.*

A probable false well in the backyard, 3170 Fee Fee Road. *Photograph by the author.*

uncapped portion serving as a secret entrance or false well. It seems strange to have two wells within one hundred yards of each other.

Freedom seekers may have been secreted in the false fireplace, which was connected to the basement room with an entrance to the tunnel. The tunnel was then used to reach the creek behind the house. The freedom seekers also could have entered the tunnel directly through the false well.

The log part is associated with James McKay, a prominent explorer and Spanish government official in the area in the late eighteenth and early nineteenth centuries. It was supposedly his fort, as Natives were in the area at that time. Much of McKay's correspondence with Spanish officials is still extant, and I have examined photocopies of it. He led an expedition west and mapped out some of the area he explored. Lewis and Clark used his maps on their famous expedition that was started in 1804. The log "fort" is being moved to a Bridgeton Park. It was saved through the efforts of Jeanne Keirle, Julie Nicolai and Bridgeton government officials.

A house (1830) just north of 3170 Fee Fee Road is purported to have been an Underground Railroad safe house. The current owner says it has a tunnel that may have connected to 3170 Fee Fee Road.

ANGLUM AREA, BRIDGETON, ST. LOUIS COUNTY

Formerly enslaved people settled in this town after the Civil War. Local residents claimed the Underground Railroad operated in Anglum before the war. During the antebellum era, Bridgeton had several large tobacco farms. Anglum is now an industrial area, and the only remnant of the settlement is the name of one of the streets, Anglum Road.

FRANK MOELLERING HOUSE, FLORISSANT, ST. LOUIS COUNTY (1827–1833)

During renovations, a three-by-five-foot space containing a crock and dipper was found between the walls, a likely Underground Railroad hiding place.

Sisters of St. Joseph of Carondelet, Carondelet, St. Louis City (1841, 1858 and 1885)

The sisters came to St. Louis in 1836. They initially used a log structure. The construction of the brick building was started in 1841. When I was taking a tour of the building, the guide pointed out a hiding place under the floorboards and told us there were tunnels under the wings, both used on the Underground Railroad. There is a central spot where one can stand and see the river, where boatmen would wait to transport freedom seekers. Ironically, people enslaved by the construction company built the wings.

The sisters were known for aiding Black people from the time they arrived in St. Louis (as were the local Sisters of Mercy). They educated Black children at a time when it was illegal to teach them in Missouri. They also gave them religious sacraments. The Know Nothings (a nativist party opposed to immigrants) threatened to burn down the convent. One evening, the sisters were approached three times by a mob, and the police had to be summoned to disperse it. The mayor said he would close their school. Some of the sisters were in Mississippi during the Civil War. While on a train, they were spit on for assisting Black people. Some convent students left during the Civil War.

House near Highway 55 and Bayless, Bella Villa, St. Louis County, Missouri

The owner of the newer house on the property found a tunnel that runs from the Mississippi River, by Jefferson Barracks, up Telegraph Road, past his house and on to Carondelet Park. The tunnel is thought to have been used on the Underground Railroad. The tunnel is shown on the plans for the original house on the property. There is purportedly an entrance to the tunnel located in the basement of the Lyle mansion in Carondelet Park. The deceased former mayor of Bella Villa had the plans showing the tunnel.

Twillman House, Spanish Lake, St. Louis County, Missouri

John Henry Twillman arrived in the St. Louis area with his parents in 1842. According to Gina Seibe of Historic Florissant Inc., tunnels, some of which had caved in, were found on the property close to the Missouri River and were supposedly used on the Underground Railroad. The house was not built until 1870.

Caves underneath St. Louis City

According to the book *Lost Caves of St. Louis*, the famous cave system under St. Louis was used to hide freedom seekers. Some of these caves were used by the many breweries in the city to store beer. For example, there was a cave at the intersection of Broadway and Tyler Street used for beer storage by the brewer Kerzinger in the 1850s. The Phoenix Brewery cave is another pre–Civil War example. I am not saying these two caves were used on the Underground Railroad, but some of them probably were.

"Lemp Cottage," St. Louis City

This is an example of a house that is advertised as an Underground Railroad station but was most likely not. There is a website that details the excavations a high school teacher performed with his students at the site. He said they found artifacts from enslaved people. It would be difficult to prove they belonged to enslaved people, as there were also many free Black people in the city at that time and the items could have just as easily belonged to them. The teacher also indicated they found a tunnel leading from the basement at the back of the house, through the Cherokee (Lemp) cave system and to the river. The tunnel was supposedly used by freedom seekers, including those who had been enslaved by the DeMenil family. However, according to the former director of the nearby DeMenil mansion, the family never held enslaved people at that location.

Hoppe Mansion, St. Louis City (Circa the Early 1850s)

An 1853 plat map of the mansion shows a trapdoor in the basement floor with stairs leading to the lower level, where there was also a trapdoor. Under the second trapdoor was a brick-lined room leading to a cave (Cherokee Cave ran underneath the Lemp neighborhood). A man who lived in the area for many years indicated this room was used on the Underground Railroad. This basement area was intact and used as a speakeasy in the late 1920s.

Lyle Mansion, Carondelet Park, Carondelet, St. Louis City (1859–75)

An elderly resident of Carondelet noted that a tunnel led from the basement of the house to the Mississippi River. Other area houses and places around Jefferson Barracks were involved in this Underground Railroad route, which, at one time, used Dan's Ferry to cross the Mississippi River to Illinois.

Ebenezer Chapel, St. Louis City (1845)

According to its 2005 National Register of Historic Places nomination, this church was built for abolitionist Methodists, who welcomed free and enslaved Black people as members. They carried arms to protect themselves from Southern sympathizers. Although the church is not mentioned as an Underground Railroad station, it does have a history of assisting the city's Black population.

Schoelhorn-Albrecht Building, 721–23 North Second Street, Laclede's Landing, St. Louis City (Pre-1844)

The building was originally used by the Schoelhorn-Albrecht Machine Company to manufacture capstans for barges and steamboat engines and

An Underground Railroad hiding place under the sidewalk by the former Morgan Street Brewery. *Photograph by the author.*

deck equipment for boats used during the 1849 California gold rush. At one time, German abolitionists owned the building and ran it as a tavern. An interior door in the north wall opened to a cellar and tunnel. The transom window over it was at street level. The cellar room is under the sidewalk on Morgan Street, between Second Street and Collins Alley. The tunnel utilized a natural cave that went all the way to the Mississippi River. The building's most recent tennant was the Morgan Street Brewery.

Mary Meacham Freedom Crossing and John Berry and Mary Meachum House, St. Louis City

The Mary Meachum Freedom Crossing is on the National Park Service's National Underground Railroad Network to Freedom. Mary Meachum was born into slavery in Kentucky in 1801. Around 1815, her husband bought her freedom in St. Louis. She was married to John Berry Meachum, a prominent preacher and educator. They were both Underground Railroad conductors and also purchased enslaved people in order to free them.

In 1855, Mary and Isaac, a free Black man, tried to ferry freedom seekers across the Mississippi River to Illinois. They were caught and charged with

John Berry Meachum's grave in Bellefontaine Cemetery. *Photograph by the author.*

the theft of enslaved people under the 1850 Fugitive Slave Act. The charges against Isaac were dropped. The *Missouri Republican* reported that Mary was tried by a jury and acquitted of at least one charge, with the remainder eventually dropped.

Mary Meachum's cenotaph on John Berry Meachum's grave. *Photograph by the author.*

The Meachums' house at 136 North Second Street in St. Louis City served as an Underground Railroad safe house. It was demolished long ago, and the area is now the site of railroad tracks and industrial development. After John died, Mary continued with their work. The Freedom Crossing has a small museum and a wonderful mural by local high school students across the path from it.

John Berry Meachum taught Black students on a boat moored in the Mississippi River, a neutral area, since it was illegal to teach Black people in Missouri (beginning in the 1840s). He also conducted the Candle Tallow School, which met in the basement of Meachum's First African Baptist Church.

An 1864 *Daily Missouri Democrat* article described Mary. She was the president of the Colored Ladies Soldiers' Aid Society in St. Louis, also known as the Colored Ladies Contraband Society, an organization of free Black women formed in 1863 to assist Black Union soldiers and freedom seekers. They took care of the segregated wing of Benton Barracks hospital, tending to wounded Black soldiers. To get there, the women had to negotiate with a streetcar company to ride it once per week, since Black people were not allowed to ride them. A white nurse at the hospital described the members of the Colored Ladies Soldiers' Aid Society as follows: "[They are] intelligent colored women, ladies in fact, many of them well-educated and wealthy."

John Berry Meachum was buried in Bellefontaine Cemetery. Mary's inscription on the monument is a cenotaph. We do not know where she was buried.

ST. LOUIS RIVERFRONT AREA

John Johnson was an Underground Railroad conductor who was arrested for helping a freedom seeker enslaved by St. Louis attorney E.J. Gay. They were caught while trying to cross the Mississippi River at Upper Ferry (an area just north of the riverfront). Johnson was fined and imprisoned. The fate of the freedom seeker is unknown.

AFRICAN AMERICAN BARBERS OF ST. LOUIS

In St. Louis, free Black people worked as barbers, serving white clients. They knew each other and possibly worked together on the Underground Railroad. The Roberson brothers, Frank, William and Robert, were Prince Hall Masons and probably assisted freedom seekers on the Underground Railroad in conjunction with other conductors in the area, such as John Berry and Mary Meachum, who knew the Robersons. John Berry was also a Prince Hall Mason.

WILLIAM GREENLEAF ELIOT

William Greenleaf Eliot, a Unitarian minister who cofounded Washington University in 1853, was involved in freeing enslaved people. In 1860, he released an enslaved woman, Sarah Green, from Lynch's Slave Pen. Her parents had paid Eliot to rescue her. An 1854 court record indicates Eliot emancipated Amanda Holmes, a "slave for life." As mentioned earlier, Eliot and his wife, Abigail, assisted Archer Alexander in his escape from slavery in St. Charles County.

Peter and Nancy Hudlin House
(Now the Site of a Domino's Parking Lot),
Thirteenth Street, between O'Fallon and Cass,
St. Louis City (Demolished)

Peter Hudlin, a free Black man, with the help of his wife, Nancy, received freedom seekers hidden in crates on wagons at this house. They were taken to the basement and then to Alton, Illinois, during the night. There is an 1857 deed for the house. Hudlin used this "Lovejoy Line" as an Underground Railroad escape route. He was a member of the Knights of Tabor secret society, which hoped to end slavery by force of arms. The Mary Meachum Freedom Crossing, located on the Mississippi River, was nearby to the northeast.

John O'Fallon, an enslaver, had his Athlone Plantation around Grand Boulevard and Highway 70, near the north water towers. It comprised over six hundred acres. The only remnant of the plantation is a street in the area named Athlone. O'Fallon's property included today's O'Fallon Park and part of Bellefontaine Cemetery. There were other farms in the area with enslaved workers. Freedom seekers from these farms may have used the nearby Meachum and Hudlin Underground Railroad safe houses.

Joseph Nash McDowell's Medical College,
St. Louis City (1840s)

McDowell was a Southern sympathizer who fled the city during the Civil War. The Union army confiscated his medical college building at Ninth and Gratiot Streets (demolished) and turned it into the Gratiot Street Prison. According to John Rodabaugh in *Frenchtown*, freedom seekers were housed in the prison as contraband. They were allowed to leave at will and even ran errands and carried water.

St. Stanislaus Seminary (1840) and St. Ferdinand Shrine (1819–the 1850s), Florissant, St. Louis County

The convent at St. Ferdinand Shrine was built in 1819. The sisters had a reputation for assisting Black people and a mission of helping the oppressed. Although St. Stanislaus enslaved people, it is thought that Father Nerinx organized Underground Railroad activities at the seminary and shrine, according to author and scholar Father James Faherty. From the seminary, one could cross the river into Illinois. Father Faherty believed Father Nerinx had come from Kentucky to St. Louis to establish an Underground Railroad station. He asked the Sisters of Loretto at the school at St. Ferdinand Shrine to help him.

St. Stanislaus Seminary. *Photograph by the author.*

FIRST BAPTIST CHURCH, ST. LOUIS CITY

James Young was born into slavery in 1831 and converted to Christianity in 1848. He was baptized at First Baptist Church by Reverend John Berry Meachum and granted permission to preach. In 1853, Young ran away from his St. Louis enslaver and went to Chicago. After six months there, he moved on to Canada. He eventually returned to St. Louis and was named the pastor of First Baptist Church.

LEWIS BISSELL MANSION, ST. LOUIS, MISSOURI (1823)

According to Dan Fuller of Bellefontaine Cemetery, there was a cave system underneath this house that led to the Mississippi River. It was found during excavations that were done for the highway. Bissell was antislavery, and the tunnels may have been used on the Underground Railroad. Lewis was Daniel Bissell's nephew. Daniel was an enslaver.

MAP OF HARBOR OF ST. LOUIS (1837)

A map (not pictured) shows the Piper Ferry Landing in Brooklyn, Illinois. Was this where Priscilla Baltimore and other residents of Brooklyn were assisting freedom seekers from the St. Louis area? Was this where the Meachums were taking freedom seekers?[§]

MISSOURI "SLAVE STAMPEDES"

"Slave Stampede" was a phrase coined by nineteenth-century newspapers to describe a group of enslaved people embarking on a journey to freedom. The following stampedes are documented in the article "Slave Stampedes on the Missouri Borderlands."

---

§ *No. 3 Map of the Harbor of St. Louis, Mississippi River*, surveyed by Lieutenant Robert E. Lee, drawn by Lieutenant Meigs (South Washington City, MN: W.J. Stone, 1837).

In January 1850, fourteen enslaved people from St. Louis fled across the Mississippi River to Illinois. Unfortunately, a posse greedily looking for the $2,400 reward caught up to eight of them north of Springfield. One of the freedom seekers, Hempstead Thornton, swung his crutch and knocked three posse members unconscious. Five of the freedom seekers were recaptured but managed to successfully escape. The Illinois Supreme Court ruled that Thornton was a free man and struck down an 1819 law that allowed for the recapture of freedom seekers.

In 1835, seven freedom seekers escaped from an army officer in St. Louis. The freedom seekers and two white men who helped them were recaptured in Illinois. The white men were taken back to Missouri and beaten by a proslavery mob.

Around 1849, John and Lucinda Henderson and their two children ran away from St. Louis. They were helped across the Mississippi River by a white woman, Susan Yates. They then went on foot to Alton and eventually reached Chicago.

Four freedom seekers from the Iron Mountain area of St. Francois County were captured by a posse at Gravel Creek Bridge near Chester, Illinois. The two groups clashed twice, and two freedom seekers were murdered, one was badly wounded and recaptured and one escaped successfully. The corpse of one of the murdered freedom seekers, John Scott, was decapitated by a proslavery mob. A pair of white men from Illinois who opened fire on the freedom seekers were charged with manslaughter but were acquitted in 1861.

The St. Louis Slave Stampede of 1856 occurred when eight or nine Missouri freedom seekers fled the farm of Robert Wash, a retired judge, on the outskirts of St. Louis. It is possible they joined three other freedom seekers enslaved by John O'Fallon. The *St. Louis Republican* reported that "several other slaves are supposed to be in their company on the underground track." A reward of $1,500 was offered. The fate of the freedom seekers is unknown. The *St. Louis Democrat*, on July 16, 1856, noted, "Underground Railroad agents…are said to have assisted [freedom seekers]."

In 1859, five freedom seekers from Fredericktown fled and were followed by a posse, who intercepted them at Gravel Creek Bridge. One freedom seeker was murdered, but the other four escaped, although at least two were wounded. Local Illinois authorities arrested a white man from Missouri for murder, but a proslavery mob from Missouri crossed the river and there was a standoff. Under a Missouri statute, two Fredericktown residents were charged with the stealing of an enslaved person.

The Hannibal Stampede occurred when five of the eleven enslaved people of Gilchrist Porter, along with twenty to twenty-five additional freedom seekers, escaped across the Mississippi River near Hannibal to Illinois.

Wentzville, Missouri

Caves in the area were used on the Underground Railroad, which involved local Prince Hall Masons. They were connected with those in the O'Fallon, Missouri area.

Cedar Hill Hotel, Cedar Hill, Missouri (Pre–Civil War, Demolished)

This two-story wood frame structure had a basement with stone walls and a dirt floor that served as a hiding place for freedom seekers. It was demolished in the 1970s.

House on Morgan Street, Booneville, Missouri

This house in the heart of the Little Dixie region has a tunnel underneath that leads to Morgan Street. Civil War soldiers and freedom seekers may have used it.

First United Methodist Church, Washington, Missouri (Circa 1860)

John Lacks was a major contributor and preacher of this church. There was a balcony in the sanctuary where the enslaved people had to sit. (Old Bonhomme Presbyterian Church and Rock Hill Presbyterian Church in St. Louis County also had these "slave galleries.") According to the 1860 census, Lacks enslaved six people, who built the church. Although it began as a

Southern church, during the Civil War (starting in 1864), it was occupied by Union army soldiers under General E.C. Pike and served as a headquarters and hospital. They destroyed the furniture, pews and records and defaced the walls. The soldiers stabled their horses in the basement. There are a tunnel and rooms in the basement that were possibly associated with the Union occupation or used on the Underground Railroad. They are now utilized for storage.

FRANZ HERMANN–JOHN OHEIM HOUSE, KIMMSWICK, MISSOURI (1859)

Oral tradition and longtime residents indicate this house and its grounds were occupied by Union soldiers who were guarding the train trestle over Rock Creek to help prevent the advance on St. Louis by General Price's Confederate army. The house has a vaulted stone beer cellar that contained a tunnel to Rock Creek. At the time, the creek ran directly by the house (its course has changed over the years). The home is currently being rehabbed, and the stone cellar still exists. Freedom seekers would have been hidden in the Oheim cellar and then used the tunnel to get to Rock Creek, where they

The Oheim house. *Photograph by the author.*

would have taken a skiff about one-eighth of a mile to the Mississippi River, which they crossed to get to Illinois.

The caves and creeks in the area led to the Mississippi River and were used on the Underground Railroad.

House on Merchant and Main Streets, Ste. Genevieve, Missouri (Demolished)

According to a longtime resident, there was a hidden room in this home's basement that was used as an Underground Railroad hiding place.

Mount Pleasant Winery, Augusta, Missouri

A descendent of Friedrich Muench, a famous German abolitionist, journalist, author and statesman in eastern Missouri, said the Muench family owned Mt. Pleasant Winery, which was used as an Underground Railroad safe house.

Georg Muench, Friedrich's brother and a grape and wine producer, moved to Augusta in 1859. In 1863, he gathered a large group of men to rescue and free a freedom seeker who had previously been captured in the town. He participated in another similar event earlier that year.¶

Hermann, Missouri

A tour guide at the Historic Hermann Museum explained to me that the town itself was an Underground Railroad station and that any house could have potentially been involved in it. Freedom seekers went from Hermann to St. Louis and crossed the Mississippi River to Illinois, possibly from the station at what was recently the Morgan Street Brewery on Laclede's Landing. The entire town was abolitionist, so a secret Underground Railroad was not necessary.

William Berry was born into slavery in 1846 in Montgomery County, Missouri. In 1864, on the eve of the Civil War, he escaped from the farm

¶ Anita Mallinckrodt (local historian), www.muenchfamilyassociation.com.

of his enslaver, Moses Patten, on Loutre Island, across the Missouri River from Hermann (the island is now part of the mainland across the river from Hermann). Patten owned land in Loutre Township in Montgomery County and was a teacher (1860 census) and farmer (1850 and 1870 censuses). Hermann, Missouri, had a recruiting center that enlisted Black men in the United States Colored Troops in the winter of 1862–63. Some of the Black men who enlisted were freedom seekers. To get to the recruiting center, Berry traveled south toward the Missouri River, which he had to cross. Before he was able to do so, Patten captured him near Anderson's Store. Henry Clark, an enslaver, and Jack Lane (Warren County) were at the store and were asked by Patten to help bring Berry back to his farm. Berry went to work for Jack Lane for a couple of weeks before he went back to Patten's farm. Shortly thereafter, Berry successfully fled with a group of Union soldiers from Iowa who were riding through the farm. He was taken to the recruiting center at Macon, Missouri, where he enlisted as a private in Company D, Eighteenth Regiment, United States Colored Troops, for a term of three years. After participating in combat at Nashville and in Alabama, Berry died of illness in 1865.

BRAZEAU, MISSOURI

Long oral tradition says that a large cave with a natural room on the Barber family property was used as an Underground Railroad hiding place. A spring on the Hager farm was supposedly used by Natives and freedom seekers. Medicine bottles and Native tools and arrowheads were found there.

MERAMEC CAVERNS, STANTON, MISSOURI

These caverns were discovered by Jacques Renault in 1716. In the eighteenth century, they were used by the French and Spanish as a base of operations for lead and copper mining. Hazel Rowena Powell, in *Adventures Underground in the Caves of Missouri*, said that during the Civil War, the caverns were used for gunpowder manufacturing and as a "station on the Underground Railroad." William Quantrill, the notorious Missouri Southern guerrilla, and his men, under the command of General Sterling Price, were ordered to "destroy the gun powder mills and the Underground Railroad in the cave."

IRON COUNTY, MISSOURI, AND THE ARCADIA VALLEY AREA

Iron County's first federal census (1860) lists over three hundred enslaved people who were residing there. The museum and earthen work Union fort at Pilot Knob, Missouri, remains there today and is open to the public. In the Battle of Pilot Knob/Battle of Fort Davidson, the fort was attacked by Confederates, who suffered significant losses. The Union troops abandoned it during the night after blowing up its central powder magazine. It was built in 1863, with the help of a company of "contrabands," or enslaved people who had fled from slavery to Union army lines for protection, employment and freedom. Arcadia Valley was an excellent temporary hiding place for freedom seekers, with its hills, valleys and waterways. They could go behind Union lines in the area or move eastward toward the Mississippi River and Illinois.

Solomon and Moses Lax escaped slavery in 1862. Moses helped build Fort Davidson, and Solomon helped defend it during the battle. Both were buried in Park View Cemetery in Ironton, Missouri (see its section later in this book).

IMMANUEL LUTHERAN CHURCH, PILOT KNOB, MISSOURI (CIRCA 1861)

This church was probably not directly involved in the Underground Railroad, but it has a fascinating related history. It contains the original pews, baptismal font and stand and organ (in the back room). The church was used as a hospital by the Union army during the Battle of Fort Davidson/Pilot Knob. According to local tradition, the pews were put together and used as crude operating tables. To this day, there remains a large bloodstain with a bare footprint on the floor in one of the back rooms. The Union army surgeon there was Dr. Carpenter.

A telegraph record book was left behind by the Union army after they left Pilot Knob, documenting the church's role as the Union army's headquarters during the battle. Dr. Carpenter documented that a Black Union soldier was being treated at the hospital. He was hidden in a small room under the floorboards of the second back room when the Confederates approached the church. The trapdoor to the hidden room is still there.

House adjacent to Immanuel Lutheran Church, Pilot Knob, Missouri (Pre–Civil War)

According to a local historian, this home was built by the local mining company before the Civil War. It may have been the home of a mining official. It contains a hidden staircase between the walls leading from the first-floor bedroom to a room in the basement. The staircase and room were eventually sealed up. They may have been used on the Underground Railroad, considering that pro-Southerners, as well as Union sympathizers, were in the area. Immanuel Lutheran Church across the street has no basement, so a tunnel would not have connected the church and home unless the church's basement was removed at a later date.

Caledonia Wine Cottage, Caledonia, Missouri (Circa 1824)

This structure served as a hospital for both sides during the Battle of Fort Davidson/Pilot Knob in 1864. It was built by enslaved people and served as a three-story, twelve-room inn on the stagecoach line. It was an Underground Railroad station according to long oral tradition. There was a secret door in the back of the house, which has since been covered up.

Jane Thompson Alexander House, Caledonia, Missouri (Circa 1848)

There are several homes in Caledonia that were owned by enslavers and also purported to be Underground Railroad stations, most likely due to changing ownership and the divided nature of the state of Missouri before and during the Civil War.

Jane is listed on the historic marker at the house as "Caledonia's most prominent woman of means." At one time, there were chains in the basement that were used to shackle enslaved people and a tunnel that was used to transport them from the basement to the fields to work. Local historians indicate the home was, at one point, an Underground Railroad safe house, and the tunnel ran one-tenth of a mile underneath the street.

The Old Stagecoach Stop, Caledonia, Missouri (Circa 1820s)

This building served as a Union hospital for the wounded from the Battle of Fort Davidson/Pilot Knob and was rumored to be an Underground Railroad station.

The Ruggles/Evans/Dent House (Now the Caledonia Bed and Breakfast), Caledonia, Missouri (Circa 1849)

This home contained quarters for enslaved people above the keeping room (receiving room). Oral tradition says it was also an Underground Railroad safe house at one time.

Presbyterian College (Marion College), Palmyra, Missouri (1831)

The college is associated with the Underground Railroad and abolitionist activities. Nearby Hannibal was a gathering place for hunters of the enslaved.

Stone House with Four Chimneys, Pevely, Missouri (Pre–Civil War)

This large stone house with four chimneys was an Underground Railroad safe house, as were the Rankin house and Governor Thomas Fletcher house (circa 1850) in Hillsboro, Missouri. Fletcher was a Republican, Lincoln supporter and colonel in the Union army. He was also a prisoner of war at Libby Prison during the Civil War.

Arlington Inn, DeSoto, Missouri (1860)

The Arlington Inn was built as the Iron Mountain Hotel and was once known as the DeSoto Hotel. Local tradition says it served as an Underground Railroad station.

Long House, Farmington, Missouri (1833)

This Underground Railroad safe house sported a hiding place under a trapdoor in the floor. Freedom seekers from southern Missouri were hidden there and then taken to Ste. Genevieve, where they would cross the Mississippi River to Illinois.

Ezekiel Matthews House, Fredericktown, Missouri (1848)

Enslaved people built this house with bricks they made on-site. Additions in 1903 included a porch, a pair of bedrooms and a dining room. According to oral tradition, it was an Underground Railroad safe house with a false-bottomed cabinet in the kitchen that was used as a hiding place.

Morse Mill Hotel, Morse Mill, Missouri (Circa 1816)

I have not heard any established oral tradition of this site being an Underground Railroad station. There is a twenty-two-inch-wide cistern in the basement floor. A wall in the cistern served as an entrance to a tunnel that went under the road to an icehouse near the bank of the Big River. I cannot say whether the tunnel was used for the Underground Railroad or for other purposes, like hiding Civil War soldiers or alcohol during Prohibition. The hotel and icehouse still stand today. The icehouse is now a cottage. Enslaved people built the stone wall in front of the hotel.

Monaco House, Jefferson City (Late 1840s)

Oral tradition says that tunnels led from the house to the river as part of the Underground Railroad. Evidence of a tunnel was later found halfway down the river bluff.

Cemetery by the Mississippi River, Cape Girardeau, Missouri

A guide at the Moore House in Charleston, Missouri, told me that a tombstone in the cemetery slid open to reveal an Underground Railroad hiding place. The guide was from Cape Girardeau and saw it in person forty years ago.

While in the southern Missouri region, I saw in the New Madrid Historical Museum's collection a "fugitive slave gourd" that was used as a molasses jug by a freedom seeker. The freedom seeker supposedly came from Madrid Bend, Kentucky, directly across the Mississippi River from New Madrid. The guide at the museum indicated there is no documentation proving the gourd came from a freedom seeker, but it was found near a dwelling of the enslaved on the Hunter property in New Madrid.

Jen Kirn, a guide at St. Mary of the Barrens Church in Perryville, indicated that two houses on William Street in Cape Girardeau are connected by tunnels. Numerous houses have tunnels that lead to the Mississippi River. These may have been part of an Underground Railroad network.

Hannibal, Missouri

Searching for Jim: Slavery in Sam Clemens' World, by Terrell Dempsey, notes that there is evidence that enslaved people in Marion County, Missouri, were in contact with freedom seekers in Canada, Detroit and Chicago. For example, Delphia Quarles was a free Black woman in Hannibal and a "mail courier" on the Underground Railroad. By the late 1850s, couriers were able to get mail from freedom seekers back to those still enslaved in Marion County. The Marion Association, a pro-Southern vigilante group, got wind of Quarles's activities and passed the following resolution:

> *There is a certain free woman in that city* [Hannibal], *named Delphia Quarles, who has received several letters from fugitive slaves living in Chicago and has slyly distributed them among slaves of Miller Township, causing insubordination among them. Resolved, that the Committee notify said woman to leave this State in ten days, and in the event of her failure to do so, that the Committee wait upon her in due time.*

There is no further mention of Quarles in local records.

The National Park Service lists a nearby cave as being associated with Underground Railroad activities. Local lore states that Mark Twain Cave was used to hide freedom seekers.

An 1862 letter written by William Sausser of Hannibal to his brother states:

> *The General Department of the Underground Railroad is now established at the post, and in offering every facility for passengers is doing a flourishing business. Negroes are flowing in from all directions constantly and they disappear. One half of Mr. Furgua's left—the balance choose to remain yet.*

Furgua was a Marion County man listed in the 1860 slave schedule as enslaving eleven people.**

The Fifth Street Bed and Breakfast (circa the 1850s) contains a panel in its kitchen that leads to an underground area separate from the basement. It served as an Underground Railroad hiding place.

Ste. Genevieve, Missouri

Clare Casey, a ranger at the Ste. Genevieve National Historic Park, related the story of Mary Ann, a Native enslaved woman in Ste. Genevieve. She worked with a man named Celadon in assisting freedom seekers. They may have been married.

There were several known slave stampedes that occurred in the Ste. Genevieve area. The enslaved people in the area, some of them working the mines in the region, knew each other and discussed and organized group escapes across the Mississippi River to Illinois. In the 1852 stampede, five freedom seekers, Bernard, Edward, Henry, Joseph and Theodore, fled Ste.

** Frazier, *Runaway & Freed Missouri Slaves*.

Genevieve. At the same time, three other freedom seekers, Isaac, Joseph and William, left Valles Mines. The armed groups met, crossed the Mississippi River and headed for Sparta. A group of pro-Southerners from Missouri, along with a few men from southern Illinois, responding to a $1,600 reward, pursued them. Barnard, Joseph and Theodore made it to Alton, where they were seized by three local residents. The remaining freedom seekers ran across Ely Way in Jerseyville. Way tricked them into coming to his home by offering them a meal. He and a neighbor, William Scott, a justice of the peace in nearby Delhi, were armed and forced them to surrender. In St. Louis, Amadee Valle notified the St. Louis Police Department of the escape, and five officers under Lieutenant Charles Woodward were employed to collect the freedom seekers but could not find them. Meanwhile, back in Illinois, Way, Scott and the five captured freedom seekers were taken on the steamer *Altona* from Alton to St. Louis, where the freedom seekers were confined in the St. Louis County Jail.

Isaac, Joseph and Theodore were enslaved by the Valle family, and Bernard and Henry were enslaved by Lewis Bogy, a pro-Southern politician. Edward was enslaved by William Skewer, the superintendent of Valles Mines who was originally from England, and William by Jonathan Smith, who lived near Valles Mines. Antoine Janis was the enslaver of Joseph.

Wildwood, Missouri
(Borders St. Louis County to the West)

The Wildwood area was ripe for Underground Railroad activity. It contained several big farms, each with a large number of enslaved people (for Missouri at least). Creeks large enough for small boats ran through the farms to the Missouri River, which surrounded nearby Steamboat Island, Howell Island, Steamboat Springs and Monarch Landing. Freedom seekers may have used tributaries of Wild Horse Creek to access the creek itself, which flowed into the Missouri River. One unnamed tributary runs along the Coleman Slave Cemetery. Tyler's Landing was a riverboat landing for the area plantations. A road from the river to Mt. Comfort, the William Coleman house (pre-1849), was used by enslaved people to transport goods.

Slave patrols along the Missouri River in the area hunted enslaved people to earn bounties. If an enslaver could not be found, the freedom seeker was taken to Lynch's Slave Pen to be sold.

It is documented that one of Henry Tyler's enslaved people, Peter, escaped to Augusta, Missouri. Tyler told the people there to just keep Peter and give Tyler $300.

Some of the information in this book pertaining to Wildwood comes from Sally Branson and Bill Kennedy, a local historian. Churches and burial sites of the enslaved in Wildwood are discussed later in this book.

St. Charles, Missouri

According to local author and historian Dorris Keeven Franke, there is a man-made tunnel system in old town St. Charles that leads five miles west from the Missouri River. It connected churches and homes of abolitionists and was used on the Underground Railroad. It was later used by wineries for storage.

Additional Underground Railroad Stations in St. Louis

A house on the south side of Minniewood Park in the Dutchtown area of St. Louis City was the home of an abolitionist riverboat captain in the 1850s. The house may have been an Underground Railroad station. The area was the center of a German immigrant settlement.

A flounder house east of Lafayette Square on the bluff overlooking the Mississippi River had a tunnel in the basement that was purportedly used on the Underground Railroad.

The relatives of a local realtor owned a house off Conway Road, between Lindbergh and Warson Roads (Ladue, St. Louis County), that was possibly an Underground Railroad safe house (demolished).

A house in Kirkwood (St. Louis County) had tunnels in its basement that were supposedly used on the Underground Railroad. There is now a wine cellar in the basement.

There were some German-owned Underground Railroad safe houses in south St. Louis City, including some in Carondelet.

Reverend Wahl was a German Lutheran minister and Underground Railroad conductor. The basement of his home on Cherokee Street (St. Louis City) was an Underground Railroad station.

A warehouse just north of the old power plant on the Mississippi River, north of Laclede's Landing, suffered a fire in recent years. A tunnel was found underneath the building that may have been used to hide freedom seekers who were waiting to be ferried across the Mississippi River at night.

The Hoffmyer house (demolished), near the intersection of North Broadway and DeSoto Avenue, had a large archway where freedom seekers were brought into the house. The now-vacant lot has a cave that supposedly was used on the Underground Railroad.

WESTERN MISSOURI UNDERGROUND RAILROAD ACTIVITY

The *New York Times*, on February 9, 1862, reported that seventy enslaved people "made a stampede" from Buchanon County, near St. Joseph, across the Missouri River and into Kansas. They arrived in Lawrence a few days later.

In 1858, John Brown, a famous abolitionist who later died for the cause, went to Missouri with other abolitionists and liberated eleven enslaved people. He was condemned by the area press, and Missouri governor Robert Stewart offered a massive $3,000 reward for his capture.

Fort Smith in St. Joseph was built by the Union in 1861 on Telegraph Hill (now Prospect Hill). It was commanded by Colonel Robert Smith and comprised a circle of oblong earthworks with twelve cannons used to protect the Hannibal and St. Joseph Railroad and enforce martial law. A historic marker at the site is titled "A Path to Freedom: Finding Refuge Across the River." According to the marker, there is existing evidence that points to the presence of freedom seekers in St. Joseph. Local newspapers ran many advertisements seeking their return. Just north of Fort Smith, over one hundred enslaved people from St. Joseph and Buchanon County, Missouri, escaped across the frozen Missouri River into Kansas in 1862–63. Once in Kansas, many continued on to Nebraska and then Iowa—some eventually made their way to Chicago.

3

THE UNDERGROUND RAILROAD IN ILLINOIS

I n 1675, the Jesuits established a mission along the Mississippi River near Starved Rock, Illinois, to convert the Kaskaskia to Catholicism. Due to the threat of attack by Natives, they relocated farther south down the river a couple of times, ending up at a site on the River des Peres in what is now St. Louis City in 1699. The Jesuits made one final move to Kaskaskia, Illinois. They were enslavers, and it is likely theirs were the first enslaved people in Missouri and Illinois.

In 1719–20, Phillipe Renault was hired by a French company to travel to Illinois with two hundred miners to establish mines in the area. He stopped in Saint Domingue (Haiti) along the way and purchased five hundred enslaved people. They settled near Kaskaskia, Illinois. The endeavor was unsuccessful, and after a couple of decades, Renault sold the enslaved people to French settlers and returned to France. These enslaved people were dispersed throughout the region. Some worked at the southern Illinois salt springs or the lead mining areas around Ste. Genevieve, Missouri, and others worked in St. Louis.

The Underground Railroad in Illinois was extremely active and dated to at least the 1820s (e.g., Rocky Fork). Many towns and free Black communities had safe houses or routes running through them. In fact, it is difficult to name a town in Illinois that was not associated with the Underground Railroad. Researchers have identified seven main routes through Illinois, with many additional smaller paths and sub-routes dotting the region. Alton, just across the river from north St. Louis County and St. Charles County, was a prominent Underground Railroad hub. It contains many homes and churches that were involved in the Underground Railroad, including William Wade's brokerage office on East Broadway, Dr. Emil Guelich's house at the corner of East Fourth and Henry Streets and the Cartwright house on Jersey Street. There are five documented Underground Railroad stations in a seven-block area in Upper Alton. Most of them are now private homes.

The Underground Railroad in Illinois was, for the most part, organized, tight-knit and supportive. Abolitionists and conductors throughout the state cooperated to foil catchers of enslaved people, acquit their comrades who were indicted for harboring freedom seekers and elect antislavery politicians to office. For example, prominent Underground Railroad conductor Owen Lovejoy was indicted and acquitted for assisting freedom seekers and then elected to Congress.

Ruth Deters and Delores T. Saunders (see their books in the bibliography) each documented many Underground Railroad safe houses in Illinois, and most of them had at least one extant hiding place. Some Underground Railroad stations had hiding places built into them when they were originally constructed. For example, the Teft house in Delavan had a network of hiding places, including three separate cellars that could be accessed by trapdoors, hidden cubby holes in the attic and a hidden entrance in the bedroom closet that leads to a secret attic room.

A typical Illinois Underground Railroad route took the following path: Alton riverfront, Enos Apartments, Brighton, Springfield, Bloomington (Judge Davis), Princeton (Owen Lovejoy), the Chicago Loop (John Jones, a free Black tailor from Alton who eliminated the Illinois Black Codes and owned much of the loop), boat crossing of Chicago River and Lake Michigan, Cass County (Michigan), Detroit and across the Detroit River to freedom in Canada.

Wilbur H. Seibert compiled extensive correspondence with those who personally remembered and were involved in the Underground Railroad and published them in a book (see the bibliography). He also created a map of the Underground Railroad in Randolph County. One interviewee said that freedom seekers "came up the river to Chester" and then "went northeast on the state road." There were stations along the way in Eden, Oakdale, Nashville and Centralia run by Covenanters who "kept a very large depot wide open for slaves escaping from Missouri" and sent them to Chicago and then to Canada. He continued, "Scores at a time came to Sparta, [where there] was an almost constant supply of fugitives." The conductors of Randolph County had a very high success rate.

One Illinois Underground Railroad route was as follows: Allen's Landing (Missouri), cross the Mississippi River, Rockwood, Ebenezer Hollow, Sparta/Eden (Burlingame house), Coulterville/Oakdale/Nashville/Tamaroa (Root's house), Centralia, Carlyle. From Carlyle, it split, with one route going to Alton and one to Chicago.

Seibert's route covered the following places: Missouri, Chester, northeast on state road, Eden/Sparta, Oakdale, Nashville, Centralia (Covenanters), Chicago and Canada.

In her book (see bibliography), Delores T. Saunders delineates several northern Illinois Underground Railroad routes through Illinois. They are as follows:

1. Cairo to Tamaroa and then Centralia.
2. Chester or Rockwood/Ebenezer Hollow to Eden/Sparta, Coulterville, Oakdale and then Nashville.
3. These two lines merged at Centralia and went to Vandalia, Pana, Decatur, Bloomington, Pontiac, Joliet, Chicago, the Great Lakes and then to Canada. (Hiram Wilson and Erastus Childs from Galesburg met freedom seekers and helped them start new lives there.)
4. Alton to Jerseyville, Waverly, Jacksonville and then Springfield. Two separate lines formed at Springfield.
5. The Farmington route followed the Old Quincy Line (see number 7).
6. Delavan to Dillon, Elmore, Tremont, Morton, Washington, Metamora, Cazenovia, Low Point, Ronerts, Varna, Magnolia, Granville, Peru, Howell, Vermillion, Ottawa, Aurora, Chicago, the Great Lakes and then Canada.
7. The Old Quincy Line was heavily used. It traveled from Quincy to Mendon, Augusta, Plymouth, Round Prairie, Industry, Chalmers, Vermont, Scotland, Table Grove, Ipava, Bernadotte, Smithfield, Cuba, the Cuba/Fiatt junction, Canton, Elmwood, Farmington, Brimfield and then West Jersey. Or it went from Quincy to Mendon, Carthage, LaHarpe, Roseville and then to Galesburg. These lines met at Osceola and then went to Princeton, LeMoille, Paw Paw, Sugar Grove, Aurora, Chicago the Great Lakes and then to Canada.

8. Northern Lines:
   i. The first traveled from New Boston to Aledo, New Windsor, Andover, Geneseo and then Prophetstown.
   ii. The second went from Port Byron to Hillsdale.
   iii. The second merged with the third at Lyndon and went to Sterling, Dixon, Beloit (Wisconsin) and then Canada.
9. Smaller lines entered the Galesburg area from the Old Quincy Line (due north). One went from Industry to Macomb, Bushnell and then Galesburg, and one went from Smithfield to London Mills and then Galesburg.
10. A branch of the Illinois Central Railroad, an actual railroad, took freedom seekers from Centralia to Urbana and then to Chicago. Friendly personnel employed by the railroad would secret freedom seekers into freight cars or disguise them and seat them in passenger cars. J.J. Wante of Mendota hid freedom seekers in tall grass before placing them in Chicago, Burlington and Quincy Railroad baggage cars headed for Chicago.

There were several towns in Iowa directly connected to the Illinois Underground Railroad. Salem was in the northeast corner of Iowa and worked closely with conductors and agents in Galesburg. Mr. Hizer was an agent in Salem. Denmark was the hub of Congregationalism in Iowa. In 1838, Reverend Asa Turner extended his ministry there from Quincy, Illinois. These conductors and agents had to be very careful, as the Iowa border was patrolled by catchers of freedom seekers.

Slave Haven, an Underground Railroad station in Memphis, Tennessee, was run by James Burkle and his family from 1855 to 1865. Freedom seekers went from there to Cairo, Illinois.

The Ursuline Sisters, African Methodist Episcopal churches and some American Baptist churches in Alton were involved in the Underground Railroad. According to researchers, in the 1830s, there was a loosely organized Underground Railroad route created by African Methodist Episcopal churches there. The Covenanters came to Illinois from Pennsylvania to establish a series of central Illinois Underground Railroad stations along a route that included Eden, Coulterville, Oakdale, Tamaroa and Nashville.

Alton was part of a network managed by free Black people that ran along the Mississippi River. Some of the free Black Underground Railroad conductors in the Alton area were Isaac Kelly, a former enslaved person from Georgia who lived near Sixth and George Streets, and James Thomas, who lived on Belle Street. The sign for their network was "Jocko the jockey." A larger house was built around Kelly's cabin, which was eventually uncovered and moved to a farm near Grafton, Illinois. While there, it had to be dismantled due to the deterioration of some of the logs.

Charles Hunter was an Alton real estate developer who founded the Hunterstown area of Alton in the 1830s. It was the first addition to Alton. Today, it is part of Alton, near St. Mary's Catholic Church. Many free Black people lived there, along with some freedom seekers. Hunter, his wife and his friend Weiglar were Underground Railroad conductors. Their route ran from St. Louis to the Alton riverfront and then to Weiglar's medicine shop (which was connected by a tunnel to William Wade's brokerage office) and through the Shields branch. Hunter had a buggy with a hiding place under the seat. Amanda Kitchell, born an enslaved woman in Memphis, was a freedom seeker who ended up in Alton. She stayed at the Franklin house, and Mrs. Hunter bought her freedom. Hunter and Weiglar worked with Mr. Shadow, a free Black man they hired to hide among the buildings on Broadway to watch out for freedom seekers arriving by boat. He would then take them to Weiglar's medicine shop at Central Avenue and Broadway, which had a coal tunnel connected to three others. The home of Dr. Emil Guelich was another nearby Underground Railroad station.

Alton was populated by free Black people as early as the 1820s. In the 1830s, some freedom seekers were absorbed by free Black communities in the area, such as Salu, Hunterstown, Rocky Fork, Wood Station, Brooklyn (Lovejoy), Africa (Locust Grove), New Philadelphia, Pin Oak and Lakeview (Pond Settlement). John Jones, from Alton, was the leader of a group of free Black people in Illinois who helped freedom seekers take flatboats across Lake Michigan. Jacksonville, Quincy, Springfield and Alton all had populations of at least one hundred free Black people, some of whom were involved in the Underground Railroad.

Eric Robinson, at the time of this publication, is writing a book on Gertrude Barlabie, an enslaved woman whose enslaver, Henry Clay of Richmond, Kentucky, was also her father. Her escape using a route through Missouri, Alton and Brighton is documented in a diary. Robinson indicates her last name was probably a pseudonym. He says there "are many references of slaves escaping from the [St. Louis] riverfront to Alton." The steamer *Altona* made thirty-minute roundtrips between Alton and St. Louis and was probably used to transport freedom seekers. Robinson continued, "Another route went from the St. Louis riverfront to Lovejoy, Illinois [now Brooklyn], between Madison and St. Clair Counties," a no-man's land where free Black people and freedom seekers lived.

It is interesting to note that many abolitionists were also interested in women's rights and education. Notice that many of the abolitionists were also founders or trustees of early women's educational institutions. In certain ways, abolitionism and women's rights went hand in hand. Also, the American Anti-Slavery Society had associated societies for women in Boston, Philadelphia and other cities, of which both free Black and white women were members. For example, Theodore Weld, who helped organize the American Anti-Slavery Society, chose seventy men to journey through Illinois to spread their beliefs. In 1847, a women's branch was organized in Farmington. Mary Blanchard, the wife of the president of Knox College in Galesburg, was the secretary, and Mary Davis of Peoria was the moderator. This group instigated a statewide antislavery petition.

Before the Civil War, even though slavery was illegal in Illinois, it still existed in the southern portion of the state, where enslaved laborers were needed to work the salt springs, which were controlled by wealthy men with political power, particularly John Crenshaw. There existed an active "reverse Underground Railroad," from which free or enslaved Black people were kidnapped and sold into slavery for profit, a lucrative enterprise. It began as early as 1816. In 1825, the Act to More Efficiently Prevent Kidnapping was passed but was not effective. Freedom seekers in the Cairo and Chester areas were especially susceptible to the kidnappers. This reverse Underground Railroad had agents to transport the kidnapped people out of the state. These kidnappers included Joe O'Neil (Hamilton County), Abe Thomas and "Mr. C." (Shawneetown), who had a cave on the Wabash River where he imprisoned captured people who were awaiting shipment south on Ohio River steamboats. James Duncan, Joseph McAdams and Mose Twist were kidnappers operating in the St. Louis area. Free Black people in Illinois had to carry "freedom papers." All a kidnapper had to do was confiscate their papers and tear them up, and they were at the kidnapper's mercy.

Sherwood, from Missouri, was a catcher of freedom seekers. In 1851, he attempted to catch freedom seekers in Sparta, Illinois, but was met with armed resistance and fled the scene.

The infamous John Crenshaw house (Hickory Hill) in Equality, Illinois, was built by him in 1838. He owned salt springs in southern Illinois and, along with other mine owners, leased enslaved people from Kentucky to work the mines. Much research has been done on Crenshaw and his house, with two schools of thought emerging. One says the upper floor of the house was a jail and breeding area for enslaved people, and the other says there is no evidence to support this. Photographs of the upper floor (the house is still standing) clearly show cell spaces. In her book *Illinois Liberty Lines: The History of the Underground Railroad*, Delores T. Saunders says:

> *One room was designed as the breeding room....In an attempt to develop a stronger strain of Negro slaves, Mr. Crenshaw purchased a male Negro, named Bob, for the exorbitant price of $800. This man had an exceptional record of breeding healthy offspring....Bob fathered approximately three hundred babies, and many...were...sold into perpetual slavery in the south.*

4

ILLINOIS UNDERGROUND RAILROAD SITES

QUINN CHAPEL AFRICAN METHODIST EPISCOPAL CHURCH, BROOKLYN (LOVEJOY), ILLINOIS

In 1829, Reverend William Paul Quinn organized the residents of Brooklyn to work on the Underground Railroad. Directly across the Mississippi River from St. Louis, Brooklyn was founded by Priscilla Baltimore in the 1820s. She brought eleven freedom seekers there from St. Louis. The church served as an Underground Railroad safe house. Reverend Quinn took "Mother" Baltimore to Alton and organized the Lower Alton African Methodist Episcopal Church. They then traveled to Rocky Fork and organized freedom seekers to form the Rocky Fork Bethel African Methodist Episcopal Church, thus establishing an Underground Railroad route from St. Louis to Jersey County, Illinois, via the Lower Alton African Methodist Episcopal Church and Rocky Fork.

ANTIOCH BAPTIST CHURCH, BROOKLYN (LOVEJOY), ILLINOIS (ESTABLISHED 1838)

This church was founded in 1838 and worked in conjunction with Quinn Chapel African Methodist Episcopal Church on the Underground Railroad (see previous section).

ENOS APARTMENTS (NATHANIEL HANSON HOUSE), ALTON, ILLINOIS (CIRCA 1857)

This house was designed specifically for use as an Underground Railroad station in 1857 by owner and Underground Railroad conductor Nathaniel Hanson, a farm implements salesman. His Underground Railroad activities are documented in family memoirs. The third floor and side wing were added in 1911.

The basement walls were made eighteen inches thick to muffle noise. The cupola was used to signal agents on the Alton riverfront, as there were freedom seeker hunters on the Missouri side of the Mississippi River. One light meant all was safe, and two meant there was danger. There is a tunnel in the basement that leads to the carriage house. Oral tradition states that there was a tunnel that led from the carriage house to the riverfront. A local

The Hanson house (now the Enos Apartments). *Photograph by the author.*

The basement coal storage room that served as an Underground Railroad hiding place, Hanson house (now the Enos Apartments). *Photograph by the author.*

tour guide indicated most of this tunnel has collapsed, but a portion still exists under a covered parking lot below the house. The tunnel from the basement of the main house to the carriage house is still there. The entrance can be seen in the basement.

The tunnel in the basement of the Hanson house (now the Enos Apartments) that leads to the detached carriage house. *Photograph by the author.*

Freedom seekers were hidden in a room in the basement with an arched ceiling. The walls are made of brick and limestone, and the floor is composed of dirt and rough limestone. The room extends outward from the house to the center of Third Street. According to local Underground Railroad

The carriage house at the Hanson house (now the Enos Apartments). *Photograph by the author.*

historian Eric Robinson, this room was the coal shed (soot is still visible on the walls). The only alterations made to the coal bin since it was built were the additions of electricity, water lines and a door frame. From here, freedom seekers were moved up the hill to Isaac Kelly's cabin. From there, they would continue on to the Topping house or Union Baptist Church (1837) at the corner of Seventh and George Streets, which had a nook in its basement behind a heavy steel plate that served as a hiding place. They may have then followed the railroad tracks to the Mississippi River near Brighton, twelve miles from Alton. A tunnel led from the river to the town. From there, they were secreted to Chicago and crossed Lake Michigan to Detroit, where they took the Detroit River to Canada.

Freedom seeker Mary Jane Otey was smuggled across the frozen Mississippi River into Madison County, Illinois, on the Underground Railroad. She was hidden in the coal shed at the Hanson house (this information came from Mary Ann Clark, Otey's great-granddaughter).

Boone-Kelly Cabin, Alton, Illinois (Circa the 1830s)

This hand-hewn log structure was built by Samuel Boone, a relative of Daniel Boone who had arrived in Alton with his wife, Sarah, from Pennsylvania. The cabin had a dirt floor, which was replaced with a plank floor placed over new timber joints around 1838. In 1855, Isaac Kelly, a former enslaved person from Georgia and a Prince Hall Mason, moved into the cabin after it was sold by Boone. Kelly was a teacher in Alton. The cabin was inhabited by members of the Kelly-Blodgett family for generations. A newer house was later built around the cabin, and it was soon forgotten. Robert St. Peters, a local preservationist, found the cabin in 1974. According to a May 12, 2021 telephone call with the current owner of the cabin, it was slated to be burned down and replaced by a Veterans of Foreign Wars hall. The cabin sat in St. Peters's backyard for many years until the current owner bought it for several hundred dollars. The cabin's current owner dismantled the logs and took them to his farm in Grafton, Illinois, where he reassembled them. Several logs eventually deteriorated, and the cabin had to be dismantled.

Kelly's cabin was a stop on the Underground Railroad, probably the stop after Enos Apartments. He organized escapes in conjunction with the Wood River Baptist District, an area of early Black churches, and the Prince Hall Masons. He also organized the Brothers of Friendship, a fraternal organization devoted to Underground Railroad activities. The route Kelly used, which ran from his home and roughly along the Illinois River to Springfield, was called the North Star route in honor of the Masonic lodge in Chicago. He was assisted by John Matlock, who had successfully fled from his enslaver in Missouri. Kelly was later entrusted with the secret burial of Elijah Lovejoy.

Elijah Dimmock House
(Second Reading Book Store), Alton, Illinois (1831)

This Federal-style structure was built on land owned by Rufus Easton, the founder of Alton. It was originally a dry goods store and was purchased by Elijah Dimmock in 1840. He was an Underground Railroad conductor, and the building was a safe house. He built a windowless room in the back of the building to be used as a hiding place. He moved freedom seekers to Godfrey and then along Little Piasa Creek to Brighton. The building is now the Second Reading Book Store.

The Dimmock house (now the Second Reading Book Store). *Photograph by the author.*

JAMES HENRY JOHNSON HOUSE, ALTON, ILLINOIS

Freedom seekers arrived here from points to the south, including Carlyle, Illinois. Johnson had lived in Alton since 1837 and purchased a farm there in 1854. *Towns and Families of Randolph County, Illinois*, published by the Randolph County Genealogical Society, describes the hiding place in a home that may have been Johnson's as follows: "[The house] has a room enclosed in glass, that was used for a beehive for making honey. Behind this room was a secret room in which they sheltered run-away slaves....This may have been the Johnson home." The book goes on to say that Randolph County, Illinois, had around thirty Underground Railroad safe places, including barns, homes and natural features.

HURLBUT-MESSENGER HOUSE, UPPER ALTON, ILLINOIS (1841, DEMOLISHED)

This home was located in Upper Alton, the site of several other safe houses. Freedom seekers were hidden in the large basement. A resident of the house in the early 1900s found a tunnel in the basement, which led, according to oral tradition, to the Old Rock House, another nearby safe house. The Hurlbut-Messenger house was demolished in 1957, and Calvary Baptist Church is now on the site.

NEW BETHEL AME CHURCH, ALTON, ILLINOIS

Erastus Green and George Hindman assisted freedom seekers at this church.

LOWER ALTON AFRICAN METHODIST EPISCOPAL CHURCH, ALTON, ILLINOIS (1844)

This church was organized by Reverend Quinn in 1839. He and Priscilla Baltimore established an Underground Railroad route from St. Louis through Jersey County, Illinois. The church building sheltered freedom seekers. A new church called Campbell Chapel was constructed here in 1867 (still extant). Today, it is part of Trinity African Methodist Episcopal Church. The Black churches in Alton, including this one, were involved in Underground Railroad activities.

CAPTAIN LEYHE HOUSE, ALTON, ILLINOIS (CIRCA 1860S)

This house was designed by locally famous architect Lucas Pfeifenberger and is located in the Christian Hill area of Alton, which was very active on the Underground Railroad. Captain Leyhe worked for the Eagle Packet Company on the route from Peoria to Cape Girardeau. A local resident indicated that Captain Leyhe and Pfeifenberger worked together to transport captured Confederate soldiers back to the South for profit, and they helped freedom seekers travel upriver. There is a cubbyhole in the back stairwell that was possibly used to hide soldiers and freedom seekers.

LUCAS PFEIFENBERGER HOUSE, ALTON, ILLINOIS

Pfeifenberger had a tunnel from his home to his stable in the backyard. The tunnel is rumored to still be there. Many homes in the area had tunnels.

OLD ROCK HOUSE, ALTON, ILLINOIS (1834–35)

This home was built for the Reverend T.B. Hurlbut, the pastor of the Upper Alton Presbyterian Church, a friend of Elijah Lovejoy and a teacher at Shurtleff College. The house served as an inn and was frequented by the students and faculty of nearby Shurtleff College, who were involved in Underground Railroad activities. It was also an Underground Railroad safe house and site of the organization of the Anti-Slavery Society of Illinois in 1837.

There were two fireplaces at each end of the basement. One fireplace contained a tunnel that led south to the ravine behind the house. The other contained a tunnel to the Bock house. Freedom seekers were hidden in a

Left: The Old Rock House. *Photograph by the author.*

Below: The basement of the Old Rock House. *Public domain.*

warming oven in the base of one of the chimneys. The tunnels were sealed when Clawson Street was laid.

Eric Robinson tells the story of Harry, an enslaved man from Milton, Illinois, who fled on the Underground Railroad around 1820 and was hidden in the Old Rock House. His relatives escaped to Canada via the Quincy and Chicago Underground Railroad. Robinson explained that the creeks and rivers in the Alton area, including Piasa Creek, Wood River and Pearl Creek, which went from West Alton to Upper Alton, were used to transport freedom seekers on the Underground Railroad.

BOCK HOUSE, UPPER ALTON, ILLINOIS (CIRCA 1820S)

Freedom seekers came here from the Old Rock House via what are now Clawson and Judson Streets.

SALEM BAPTIST CHURCH, ALTON, ILLINOIS

This congregation was organized in 1819, and its original church was located by the McCoy Family Cemetery. The current church, the third, was built in 1912 on Seiler Road. Some enslaved people by the name of Stuart were buried in the McCoy Family Cemetery but were later moved to the Salem Baptist Church Cemetery (1903). The McCoy Family Cemetery is still there, off a rural road and hidden in a grove of trees, with ancient yucca plants guarding the graves. This church is located right in the middle of an Underground Railroad hub and could certainly have been involved in the Underground Railroad's activities. James and Matilda Ballinger, a free Black couple from Wood Station, were buried in Salem Baptist Church Cemetery. They had seventeen children when they arrived in Illinois from Missouri.

UPPER ALTON PRESBYTERIAN CHURCH (NOW THE FORMER COLLEGE AVENUE PRESBYTERIAN CHURCH), ALTON, ILLINOIS

This church was organized in 1837 and is now located across the street from the Old Rock House. Elijah Lovejoy was its first pastor. The current building was dedicated in 1927. It is thought that the Old Rock House and Upper Alton Presbyterian Church worked together on the Underground Railroad. A house to the north of the Old Rock House was a safe house on the Methodist Line. There were Baptist, Methodist and Presbyterian safe houses along College Avenue in the area.

PRIEST'S RETREAT (TIMMERMIERE HOUSE), UPPER ALTON, ILLINOIS (1834)

This house was the home of a priest of St. Matthew's Parish (the church that was on the site of the present First Unitarian Church) who hid freedom seekers inside the house. According to Eric Robinson, if a house was used for religious purposes, it was not appropriate to look for freedom seekers there. The home was designed by Robert Debow in the form of a cross, with a veranda and floor-to-ceiling windows. The first Catholic mass in the town was held there in 1840. Father George Hamilton established a mission on

Priest's Retreat. *Photograph by the author.*

the site, and the building was used as a retreat for priests and as a school. *The Upper Alton Home & History Tour* booklet (1997) notes that "this home was reportedly one of the stations of the Underground Railroad" and had several hiding places in the basement.

Loomis Hall (Now Alton Museum of History and Art), Alton Seminary/Alton College/Shurtleff College, Alton, Illinois (1832)

Close to the Old Rock House and Upper Alton Presbyterian Church, this building was originally the academic hall, administration building and library for what would become Shurtleff College, established in 1827 in St. Clair County, Illinois. The oldest part of Loomis Hall, originally the chapel and now the front room, dates to 1832. A staircase underneath the parlor led to the cellar, which was an Underground Railroad hiding place.

Loomis Hall. *Photograph by the author.*

THE HOUSE ACROSS THE STREET FROM ST. MARY'S CATHOLIC CHURCH, ALTON, ILLINOIS

The Machen family recently discovered a circa 1840 brick tunnel under the sidewalk by the house. The brick-lined street was laid in 1895 and covered the entrance to the tunnel. The house was built in 1890, and there was no house there in 1863. The tunnel is nine feet tall, nine feet wide and at least sixty feet long. An 1860s Ruger Bird's-Eye View map and drawing shows a structure above the tunnel. As more research is done by the family, perhaps an Underground Railroad connection will be uncovered.

FIRST UNITARIAN CHURCH, ALTON, ILLINOIS (FOUNDATION CIRCA 1855)

This church was built on the foundations of an older Catholic church. Author and historian Troy Taylor found a room in the left-back corner of the basement crawl space. It is not on the floor plans and is made of the same stone as the foundation. Oral history suggests the older church was an Underground Railroad station.

MONTICELLO WOMEN'S SEMINARY (NOW LEWIS AND CLARK COMMUNITY COLLEGE), ALTON, ILLINOIS

The seminary's students and faculty were abolitionists, and tunnels exist underneath the campus structures.

ALTON AFRICAN BAPTIST CHURCH (UNION BAPTIST CHURCH), ALTON, ILLINOIS (1854)

In 1836, ten African Americans, some free and some arriving via the Underground Railroad, met at Charles Edwards's house and established the African Freedmen Mission, which led to the founding of the church and school in 1837. It was organized on the encouragement of James Mason

Union Baptist Church. *Photograph by the author.*

Peck, the cofounder of Shurtleff College, who provided teachers for the school. It was part of the Underground Railroad.

The original church, a two-story wood frame building, was constructed in 1854. Alton's first Black school was located on the first floor, and the church was on the second floor. The building was sold in 1876, and a new brick church was built across the street in 1902.

SALU, IN UPPER ALTON, ILLINOIS

Salu began in the 1820s as a free Black community that absorbed freedom seekers. The residents of Salu interacted with the free Black people in Wood Station, like the Johnsons and Ballingers, who attended Salem Baptist Church.

Kendall Cracker Factory, Alton, Illinois (1864)

This factory is on the site of the First Baptist Church (1832), an Underground Railroad station, which was destroyed by fire. The remains of its bell tower are located in the basement of the 1864 building.

Joesting House, Alton, Illinois

The original log cabin is inside the current house (where the kitchen is). There is a long oral tradition that says the cabin was an Underground Railroad station.

Samuel Wade House, Alton, Illinois (Circa 1850s)

Wade was an abolitionist carpenter who arrived in Alton from Maine in the 1830s. The home's current owner says the house was most likely an Underground Railroad station. It is located in Middletown, an area that was active on the Underground Railroad. The house had several additions, including a kitchen (the 1880s), a two-story porch (the 1940s) and a modern rear addition.

Other Alton Sites Associated with the Underground Railroad

Oral tradition indicates that the following sites were also involved in Underground Railroad activities: the James P. Thomas house (on Belle Street, the post office is there now) and the Ursuline Convent and School (1859). Construction workers in the 1930s found a hidden room under the main floor of the convent that could only be accessed through a trapdoor.

Wood Station, Illinois

The free Black families in Wood Station, including the aforementioned Johnsons and Ballingers, helped absorb freedom seekers into the community or assisted them on to the next station.

Bridge over the West Branch of Wood River Creek (Shipman Road, Now Wood Station Road), Wood Station, Illinois

John M. Palmer was the conductor at this station.

Brighton, Illinois

Dr. Thomas Brown's house in Brighton was the next safe house after Wood Station. He hid freedom seekers in his house or in an attic over a shed. Dr. Brown worked on the Underground Railroad in conjunction with his in-laws, Peter and Cherokee Van Arsdale, who lived across the railroad tracks. Freedom seekers were taken from here to Chicago via Springfield. Dr. Brown also worked in conjunction with the Palmers, who had a tunnel from the basement of their house (1828, demolished), which served as a tavern and stagecoach stop. They hid freedom seekers in the cellar.

Other Brighton safe houses included the Hill house, Herman Grigg's house and Andrews's house, which had a small cistern under the kitchen floor that was used as a hiding place. John Hart took freedom seekers from his home to Carlinville. From there, they moved on to Rocky Fork, Otterville and Carollton.

Cheney Mansion, Jerseyville, Illinois (1827)

The Cheney house was built in 1827, when the area was called Hickory Grove, a tiny settlement with three log cabins. It had two upstairs rooms and two downstairs. It was the first wood frame house in the area. In 1830, it served as a tavern and stop on the Alton–Jacksonville stagecoach line. It was known as the "Little Red House." In 1839, Dr. Edward Darcy, the owner, converted it back into a private residence. He later gave it to his daughter and her husband, the Cheneys. The newer portion of the home was built around the original structure in the 1870s. The historic marker outside the house notes, "It was also a stop on the Underground Railroad. Slaves were hidden in a false cistern in the basement accessed from a livery stable across the street via an underground tunnel." The false cistern is still there. A dumbwaiter (now gone) in the dining room was used to send food and water down to them. The Cheneys were Underground Railroad conductors and were never caught for their activities. This station may have been an intermediary stop between Alton and Jacksonville. No evidence of the tunnel remains. In 1946, the highway in front of the house was undergoing repairs when a cave-in revealed the tunnel under the road. The stagecoach line from Alton to Jacksonville, which ran by the Cheney mansion, was used to transport freedom seekers. The buggies either had hiding places under their front benches, or the curtains in the passenger compartment were kept closed. The complex contains other historic structures and is available for tours.

White Cabin, Jerseyville, Illinois (1828)

The cabin of Joshua White, near Jerseyville, was built by him in 1828. He hid freedom seekers in the rafters under the tin roof.

Dr. Benjamin Franklin Long's Farm (Sylvan Grove), Godfrey, Illinois

Dr. Long founded the Illinois Mutual Fire Insurance Company, a legitimate business that served as cover for an Underground Railroad network through central and northern Illinois. His farm was the first stop on the system around Rocky Fork.

Benjamin Roots House, Tamaroa

Roots was a surveyor for the Illinois Central Railroad from 1830 to 1840 and had tracks built through the front yard of his Kinsey Crossing farm. The tracks were completed in 1856. He also built a private depot. He hid freedom seekers in sealed freight cars bound for Chicago. He hid them in the cistern until they could be transferred to the freight cars. His home had secret passages within its walls that led to hidden rooms on the second floor and a false cistern underneath the kitchen.

William Hayes House, Sparta, Illinois

Hayes, whose home was an Underground Railroad safe house, was fined $300 for assisting a freedom seeker who belonged to Andrew Borders. He had to sell some of his land to pay the fine. His house had a space under the enclosed staircase that was used for hiding freedom seekers.

Other Sparta Underground Railroad agents included Reverend Milligan and Reverend Sloane. Mr. Evans was a conductor between Sparta and Eden. There was a colony of Covenanters, ardent abolitionists, in town. What is now the Breath of Eden Country Store (1850) was also an Underground Railroad station.

There were thirteen Underground Railroad stations in the Sparta area. The town also had a Black community in which some freedom seekers chose to settle.

Burlingame House, Eden, Illinois

This brick house sat on lots 4, 5, 6 and 7 of block 14. According to *Towns and Families of Randolph County, Illinois*, published by the Randolph County Genealogical Society, the house "was a part of the Underground Railroad." Burlingame was a prosperous businessman and constructed a large, steam-powered factory. He also owned a business that made wagons, plows and water pumps. His main market was located in Carlyle, Illinois, ninety miles from Eden and an Underground Railroad stop. He used this business as a cover for his Underground Railroad work. He built feed boxes into his wagons that had false compartments for concealing freedom seekers.

Covenant Church, Eden, Illinois (Circa 1819)

This antislavery reformed Presbyterian church was founded in 1819. The church led the area's Underground Railroad network. There is a court record that indicates a church member, a farmer in the Eden-Sparta area, helped an enslaved mother and her children in 1842. Unfortunately, she was apprehended.

Dr. Hiram Rutherford House, Oakland, Illinois

Rutherford was a friend of Abraham Lincoln. His home was an Underground Railroad safe house. He was involved in the Matson slave trial (1847), in which it was decided whether enslaved people living in the area were free. The judge ruled in favor of the enslaved people, and a Black community eventually formed in the area.

Old Stone House, Coulterville, Illinois (Mid-1800s)

This house was the home of the town founder, James Coulter, and served as an Underground Railroad station.

John Hood House, Oakdale, Illinois (1843)

This Underground Railroad station was built by John Hood, a Covenanter. The Covenanters comprised a Presbyterian movement opposed to slavery. This house was on the Underground Railroad route that started in Chester and went northeast through Randolph, Washington and Marion Counties. The Oakdale Cemetery contains the graves of people associated with the Underground Railroad. The site of the Todd house is nearby. Reverend Andrew Todd was an Underground Railroad conductor and pastor of the Presbyterian church in Oakdale, which was located next to the cemetery. Other Oakdale conductors included John B. Carson, Cyrus McClurken (a driver), John Torrens (a driver), John B. and Donaldson. They lived on farms around the cemetery.

A blacksmith shop owned by Robert Smith was on the John Hood property before he moved there and served as an Underground Railroad safe house around 1843.

Marissa, Illinois

Local oral tradition indicates Marissa was an Underground Railroad stop with a series of safe houses. One of them belonged to Matthew Hamilton on Bess Street.

"Emancipation Baptists," Also Known as Baptized Churches of Christ, Friends to Humanity, in Southern Illinois

These congregations maintained friendly relationships with Black Americans, and the first church was organized in 1809. Antislavery missionaries established churches across southern Illinois, including the Colored Emancipated Church in Shawneetown, with fifteen Black members, and Bethel Church, near Collinsville, an Underground Railroad station. Some of these churches participated in Underground Railroad activities.

Rockwood (Liberty)/Ebenezer Hollow Area, Illinois

Dr. William Vance gave medical assistance to freedom seekers, and the local women fed and clothed them. They were taken through Ebenezer Hollow to the area of a cave and hide tannery, which served as a cover for Underground Railroad activities. From there, they went to the Burlingame house in Eden, Illinois.

Although the Underground Railroad was active in the area before 1850, an abolitionist group was formed around that year in Rockwood and headed by Ezekial Barber. He met freedom seekers and gave them food. He then took them to William Harry's home, where they were hidden in the cellar. Harry was a cobbler and justice of the peace. He made new shoes for the freedom seekers. His house was built against a bluff, and when freedom seeker hunters arrived, he moved the freedom seekers from the cellar to small recesses in the bluffs.

First Presbyterian Church in Rockwood and Ebenezer Presbyterian Church near Rockwood were involved in Underground Railroad activities. Route 3 crosses Mary's River near Rockwood. The river was followed by freedom seekers from where it begins at the Mississippi River, just below Chester, Illinois, an Underground Railroad hub, almost all the way to Chicago. From Chester, freedom seekers went along the Mary's River to the Eden/Sparta area.

The graves of descendants of James Clendinen, an area Underground Railroad conductor, are located in Ebenezer Memorial Cemetery near Ebenezer Presbyterian Church. Clendinen arrived in Chester in 1837 and used a cave on his farm as a hiding place.

Allen's farm was located across the Mississippi River from Rockwood. It was referred to as Allen's Landing and was worked by enslaved people. A trade network existed between Allen's Landing and the merchants of Rockwood. George, one of Allen's enslaved people, was allowed to take goods across the river. He used this as a cover to transport freedom seekers across the river to Rockwood.

I have also heard stories about Liberty Island in the Mississippi River near Chester being used as a resting place for freedom seekers. It no longer exists as an island.

Old Landmark Inn, Chester, Illinois (1830s)

In 1838, the stone portion of this house was owned by Thomas Mather and used as a store or warehouse. A second story was added in 1892. It served as an Underground Railroad station, with a tunnel that led from the home to the river.

Halliday Hotel, Cairo, Illinois

This Underground Railroad safe house had hidden rooms in its basement.

George Burroughs, a Black porter for the Illinois Central Railroad, was an Underground Railroad agent. He moved freedom seekers on the railroad from Cairo to Chicago. Per a letter transcribed in 1896, Burroughs hid a female freedom seeker on a freight train at "St. Louis Junction" (near Centralia) in the 1850s.

As documented in the 1850s court case *Rodway v. Illinois Central Railroad*, a free Black woman from Cairo helped freedom seekers purchase a ticket north on the Illinois Central Railroad.

SHAWNEE NATIONAL FOREST, ILLINOIS

Freedom seekers found their way through this forest, which included the free Black community of Miller Grove. Four families from Tennessee settled the area. The Miller grove community assisted freedom seekers. Natural landmarks in the forest that served as hiding places included Sand Cave, Crow Knob, Brasher Cave, Fat Man's Squeeze and Ox-Lot.

DR. RICHARD EELS HOUSE, QUINCY, ILLINOIS (1835)

In 1840, Reverend John Cross arrived in Quincy to survey locations for Underground Railroad safe houses from there to Chicago. He was considered the superintendent of the Underground Railroad (he was succeeded by Owen Lovejoy).

It is estimated that the Eelses helped two hundred to four hundred freedom seekers through Quincy. Richard and his wife, Jane, helped get them to Woodlawn Farm in Jacksonville via their home and the Mission Institutes. They built their house in 1835 on the bluffs four blocks from the Mississippi River. Dr. Eels was elected president of the Adam's County Anti-Slavery Society in 1839. In 1842, Berryman Barnett, a former enslaved man and one of Quincy's first known Underground Railroad agents, brought Charley, a freedom seeker, to the Eelses' residence. They were intercepted by a posse on their way to the Mission Institute. Charley ran across Madison Square Cemetery but was captured and returned to Missouri. Dr. Eels was charged with harboring a freedom seeker, tried, found guilty and fined $400 by Judge Stephen A. Douglas, who would later gain fame as Lincoln's opponent in their series of political debates in Illinois. Dr. Eels was president of the Illinois Anti-Slavery Party in 1843 and candidate for the Liberty Party

The Eels house. *Photograph by the author.*

in the 1844 presidential election. That same year, the Illinois Supreme Court rejected Dr. Eels's appeal. He died at the age of forty-six on a steamboat on the Ohio River on his way east for rest. In 1852, the estate of Dr. Eels appealed his case to the United States Supreme Court, which upheld the guilty verdict. This was the only documented Underground Railroad case to be heard in that court. William Seward and Salmon Chase, future members of President Lincoln's cabinet, represented Dr. Eels in his U.S. Supreme Court case. In 2015, Illinois governor Pat Quinn granted a full pardon to Dr. Eels. The hiding place for freedom seekers, a small space off the basement in the front of the house, was recently discovered.

MISSION INSTITUTES NOS. 1–4, QUINCY, ILLINOIS

Mission Institute No. 1, at Sixty-First Street and Broadway, was established on eighty acres of land in 1838 by Dr. David Nelson, a staunch abolitionist and Underground Railroad conductor. Dr. Nelson purchased the property and built a chapel, twenty log cabin dormitories and a sawmill on it. His home was nearby, at Sixtieth and State Streets. He conveyed the land in trust to Reverend Asa Turner to organize a manual labor missionary college, Mission Institute No. 1, or Adelphia Theological Seminary. It was open to both men and women, a radical notion for the day. In the late 1830s, students, including William Bird, William Mellen and N.A. Hunt, served as Underground Railroad agents.

Mission Institute No. 2, or Theopholis, located on eleven acres at Twenty-Fourth and Maine Streets, was a manual labor institute founded by Dr. David Nelson and Dr. Richard Eels in 1836. Dr. Nelson was a Presbyterian minister who freed his enslaved people in Virginia and moved to Palmyra, Missouri, where he founded Marion College. He was soon driven out by pro-Southerners and moved to Quincy, where he became pastor of the Lord's Barn. Mission Institute No. 2 was run by Reverend Moses Hunter. The Benjamin Terrell house on the property served as a four-room dormitory and hiding place for freedom seekers. Freedom seekers were hidden between the second-story floor and first-story ceiling and in a secret room in the basement that was accessible only through a trapdoor. Underground Railroad agents there included Alanson Work, Burr, George Thompson, Lewis Andrews, John Rudyard, George and Andrew Hunter, Edward Griffin, William Mullen and Reverend H.D. Platt. In 1843, a mob from Marion City, Missouri, crossed the Mississippi River and burned the school to the ground because it allowed Black students to study there.

The location of Mission Institute No. 3 is not known. It may have been planned for a "seminary lot" for a school that is visible on an 1837 plan of Payson, Illinois.

Mission Institute No. 4 was a forty-acre landing place for freedom seekers in the southwest corner of Melrose Township, six miles south of Quincy, near Turtle Lake. They arrived by crossing the Mississippi River near Marion City. They could have walked across if the river was frozen or used the ferry. A buggy would then transport them to Mission Institute No. 2. Or they may have arrived via Mill Creek and Little Mill Creek. They then went north to the Turners in Quincy and Mendon.

In 1841, three students at Mission Institute No. 2, Alanson Work, James Burr and George Thompson, were caught assisting freedom seekers by Missouri authorities. They were convicted and served several years in prison at the Missouri State Penitentiary in Jefferson City.

CONGREGATIONAL CHURCH, QUINCY, ILLINOIS (ORGANIZED 1833)

This church was organized in 1833 from the Presbyterian church in Quincy. Reverend Asa Turner's icehouse at his farm, Maple Lane, was used as a hiding place for freedom seekers. In 1834, the Association of Congregational Churches was founded in his home.

SECOND PRESBYTERIAN CHURCH (NOW WESTMINSTER PRESBYTERIAN CHURCH), SPRINGFIELD, ILLINOIS (ORGANIZED 1835)

Several members of this church were involved in Underground Railroad activities, including Black conductor Jamieson Jenkins, who was a member of this church until 1851. He was a former enslaved man who gained freedom in 1846. Jenkins's house (late 1840s) was located on Eighth Street, a block from where the Lincolns lived.

In 1850, Jenkins was involved in a "slave stampede," in which he helped eleven freedom seekers from St. Louis get to Bloomington, Illinois, using the actual railroad. The St. Louis enslavers offered a $300 reward for the return of the freedom seekers.

WILLIAM DONNEGAN HOUSE, SPRINGFIELD, ILLINOIS

Donnegan was a Black shoemaker with a shop located a block east of the Abraham Lincoln–William Herndon law office. Lincoln was one of his customers. Donnegan's one-and-a-half-story house was an Underground Railroad station. Around 1908, he was lynched during the Springfield race riots.

Places in Springfield associated with Donnegan's Underground Railroad work include Converse School, African Methodist Church, Hickox Mill and his brother Preston's house.

Reverend Henry Brown, Springfield, Illinois

Reverend Brown was a Black Underground Railroad conductor in Springfield and Quincy.

Aaron Dyer, Springfield, Illinois

Dyer was a Black blacksmith and drayman who was also an Underground Railroad conductor.

Luther Ransom House, Springfield, Illinois

Ransom was an Underground Railroad conductor whose house was located near the Lincolns' residence at the Globe Tavern.

Thomas Madison Davis House, Springfield, Illinois

Davis was a freedom seeker who ended up in Springfield. He was assisted in his Underground Railroad activities by James Henderson Lee. They referred to the house as the "Young Men's Aid Society." A Black man, "Free," helped freedom seekers get to Chicago.

Zion Missionary Baptist Church, Springfield, Illinois

This congregation was founded as the Colored Baptist Church by free Black people and freedom seekers from Kentucky, Virginia and Missouri who had settled in the area two years before the city's charter in 1840. This church most likely assisted incoming freedom seekers travel north or absorbed them into the community.

OTHER SPRINGFIELD, ILLINOIS UNDERGROUND RAILROAD CONDUCTORS

Erastus Wright and Seth Conklin were also Underground Railroad conductors in the area.

ELLISON BRALEY HOUSE, CARLINVILLE, ILLINOIS (DEMOLISHED)

This home was an Underground Railroad station.

MARY PULMAN STATION, BETWEEN PAYSON AND ADAMS (NEWTOWN), ILLINOIS

This safe house is an example of a station run by a woman.

L.C. MAYNARD HOUSE, ONE MILE EAST OF LAHARPE, ILLINOIS

Maynard was an Underground Railroad conductor and LaHarpe's first merchant. Dr. Richardson and Joseph Hindman were other Underground Railroad conductors in the area.

JOHN LYMAN HOUSE, FARMINGTON, ILLINOIS

Lyman used a small cabin inhabited by Black people as an Underground Railroad safe house. Jay Slater's small brick house in nearby Gardner was also a station.

LUTHER BIRGE HOUSE, FARMINGTON, ILLINOIS

Freedom seekers went from here to either Galesburg, Stark County, Brimfield or Princeton. Birge was a carpenter and constructed a tunnel on his property to hide freedom seekers. He was indicted by a grand jury three times for harboring freedom seekers but was never convicted.

DEACON JIREH PLATT HOUSE, MENDON, ILLINOIS

Deacon Platt and his four sons were involved in Underground Railroad activities in the Mendon area. They even documented them: Jireh kept a ledger of freedom seekers' names and how many came through, and Enoch kept a journal of his activities.

OLD COLONY CHURCH, GALESBURG, ILLINOIS

This church was organized in 1837 with a combination of Presbyterian and Congregationalist members, and it first met in Hugh Conger's cabin. The first church building was completed in 1846. In his seminal 1898 account of the Underground Railroad, Wilbur Siebert identified this church as an Underground Railroad station, as did Booker T. Washington in a 1900 speech.

KNOX COLLEGE, GALESBURG, ILLINOIS (1834)

This school was founded in 1834 by Reverend George Washington Gale of New York. Its chapel and cupola were used as hiding places for freedom seekers.

NEHEMIAH WEST HOUSE, NEAR GALESBURG, ILLINOIS

West moved here in 1836 and was a member of the board of trustees of Knox College. His home was an Underground Railroad station.

TAPESTRY ROOM RESTAURANT, LEBANON, ILLINOIS (CIRCA 1850)

According to Len Adams's book *Phantoms in the Looking Glass*, there is a twelve-by-twelve-foot room at the back of the basement located under the kitchen. It has a small staircase that is original to the building. The staircase is boarded over, and the entrance to a tunnel is underneath it. The entrance is bricked up. Many of Lebanon's downtown businesses were linked by tunnels, as the town was active on the Underground Railroad.

ROCKY FORK NEW BETHEL AFRICAN AMERICAN EPISCOPAL CHURCH, ROCKY FORK, ILLINOIS

Rocky Fork was a community of free Black people and freedom seekers that dated to the late eighteenth century. Near Alton, it was a station on the Underground Railroad. Freedom seekers traveled along Hop Hollow Road in Alton to Rocky Fork and Godfrey, where there was a small Black village to hide among. Don Spaulding, a surveyor for Madison County, acquired land in the southwest portion of Godfrey known as Rocky Fork, which was inhabited by freedom seekers. He moved his sawmill there, and it served as a front to allow Black workers on the property. Spaulding started a private surveying company to establish land farther north for Underground Railroad sites. Hundreds of freedom seekers sought refuge at Rocky Fork as early as 1816. According to the National Park Service, it was one of the first stops for freedom seekers from Missouri.

The first church was built in 1863 but was burned by vandals in 1985. The current church is the second on the site. According to oral tradition, there was a message tree nearby that was used to tell freedom seekers where to go. The current Camp Warren Levis (Boy Scouts) was the site of the sawmill (circa 1853). Jim Goeken, a camp ranger, indicated that freedom

Rocky Fork New Bethel AME Church. *Photograph by the author.*

seekers coming in from the Mississippi River/Alton area used Piasa Creek, Little Piasa Creek and Rocky Fork Creek to get to Rocky Fork Church. From there, they went to Monticello Female Seminary (Lewis and Clark College). The karst topography around Camp Warren Levis, with caves and sinkholes, would have provided excellent cover for the freedom seekers.

Reverend Erasmus Green arrived in the Rocky Fork area in the 1850s. A message well on his farm was used as a landmark by freedom seekers. His home was an Underground Railroad safe house.

Louise "Lottie" Isaac (1836–circa the 1900s) was high priestess of the Rocky Fork Tabernacle No. 80 of Knights and Daughters of Tabor. Before the Civil War, this group was known as the Liberty Party and had the central purpose of operating an Underground Railroad network. After the Civil War, it became a benevolent organization for Black people.

Jacksonville, Illinois

Jacksonville has at least nine documented Underground Railroad sites, most private residences. The entire town was an abolitionist hotbed, and therefore, it was not as imperative to maintain secrecy among the townspeople. If hunters of the enslaved dared to come to town, they would have to face a small army. The town is associated with the Illinois Association, or Yale Board, which was organized in 1829 to support abolitionist activities. Jacksonville was heavily involved in the Underground Railroad from the 1830s to the Civil War. Many freedom seekers who came into town were fleeing St. Louis. Researchers believe three routes ran through town.

Africa was a community of free Black people in Jacksonville. It was bounded by West Beecher Avenue (formerly College Street), South West Street, Anna Street and South Church Street. The lynchpin of the community was Mt. Emory Baptist Church, founded in 1837. Ben Henderson, a famous conductor, and Reverend Andrew W. Jackson, the pastor of Mount Emory Baptist Church, lived there. It was active in assisting freedom seekers move north.

In the 1830s, Congregational church deacon Elihu Wolcott, Ebenezer Carter, Illinois College student Sam Willard, Illinois College professor Jonathan Turner, a Mr. Eames, David Spencer and Benjamin Henderson were all Underground Railroad leaders and had assistance from others, including Illinois College students, professors and administrators. The home of Illinois College professor David Smith was used for secret Underground Railroad meetings and planning sessions.

Illinois College was founded by the Yale Board in 1829. Its first president was Reverend Edward Beecher, Harriet Beecher Stowe's brother and a friend of Elijah Lovejoy. Beecher and Lovejoy founded the first Illinois Anti-slavery Society in Alton. Beecher Hall on the Illinois College campus was a safe house. The school is rumored to have a tunnel system underneath that is connected to other area safe houses. Illinois College and Beecher Hall are included in the National Park Service's National Underground Railroad Network to Freedom.

The Congregational church, founded in 1833 by antislavery men and women, was called the Abolition Church. Deacon Elihu Wolcott was known as the chief conductor of Jacksonville's Underground Railroad. The church's members were actively involved in the Underground Railroad as well. The site is also included in the National Park Service's National Underground Railroad Network to Freedom.

Asa Talcott House, Jacksonville, Illinois (1833/1841/1861)

Asa Talcott, a brick layer and plasterer, was a passionate abolitionist and founding member of the Congregational church, many members of which were active on the Underground Railroad. Talcott's wife, Marie, was also a conductor. They hid freedom seekers in their home, the construction of which began in 1833, with additions made in 1841 and 1861, and barn, where they hid freedom seekers underneath the hay. A tunnel connected the house to a nearby brook. Conductor Ben Henderson, a formerly enslaved person who arrived in Jacksonville in 1840, said he could count on Talcott when he needed supplies for freedom seekers. An 1844 account by a freedom seeker indicates that another freedom seeker, whom authorities were searching for, was hidden in a haystack in Talcott's barn.

Henry Irving House, Jacksonville, Illinois

Irving arrived in Jacksonville in 1842 and was an abolitionist and member of the Congregational church. According to his obituary in the *Jacksonville Daily Journal*, "For a number of years after he came to this city, he had the honor to belong to the brave band of abolitionists who did so much to help fugitive slaves to freedom....His house was more than once a refuge to the freedom seekers."

Woodlawn Farm, near Jacksonville, Illinois (1824)

The farm was started in 1824 by Michael and Jane Huffaker, who came from Kentucky. They built a cabin for themselves and cabins for four free Black families, who helped tend livestock and crops, providing cover for Underground Railroad activities. The Huffakers were members of Antioch Christian Church. The two-story home standing today was built in 1840 and contains hiding places in its walls for freedom seekers.

DR. BEZALEEL GILLETT HOUSE, JACKSONVILLE, ILLINOIS (1833)

This Greek Revival home is listed in the National Register of Historic Places and was an important Underground Railroad safe house. It was purchased by Gillett, a physician, merchant and founder of First Episcopal Church, in 1838. He was also an original trustee of the Jacksonville Female Academy, founded in 1830 (merged with Illinois College in 1903). Gillett served as a doctor for both the rich and poor during the 1833 cholera epidemic. An abandoned cabin south of the house was used to hide freedom seekers. According to oral tradition, three female freedom seekers were hiding in the cabin and rescued by Professor Jonathan Baldwin Turner of Illinois College. The Gillett house is now owned by Illinois College.

GENERAL BENJAMIN GRIERSON HOUSE, JACKSONVILLE, ILLINOIS (CIRCA 1850)

A small brick house on the property was owned by Garrison Berry, who provided shelter for Emily Logan, a freedom seeker who escaped from her enslaver, Mrs. Porter Clay. The Griersons later purchased the property. General Grierson was an abolitionist and Underground Railroad conductor. Berry's original house was incorporated into the current mansion. Grierson commanded the Tenth United States Cavalry (United States Colored Troops).

PORTER CLAY HOUSE, JACKSONVILLE, ILLINOIS (1834)

This house was built by Porter Clay, the half brother of famous politician Henry Clay, on six acres. Porter's wife, Elizabeth, owned the house, which was visited by Daniel Webster and Henry Clay. Elizabeth arrived from Kentucky with two of her enslaved people, Emily and Robert Logan. The Logans escaped and hid in the free Black section of Jacksonville known as Africa (see previous section). Unfortunately, Robert was captured and taken to Naples by carriage and then to St. Louis by steamboat. He was never heard from again. Was he sold back "down the river" into slavery, or did he escape again to a life of freedom? Emily was assisted to freedom by members of the Congregational church. The Supreme Court eventually granted her freedom. Later, the house was owned by Dr. William Sanders, a dentist and professor at Illinois College and the founder of the Young Ladies' Athenaeum in 1864.

RIVERVIEW HOUSE, ELSAH, ILLINOIS (1847)

Elsah, Illinois, is located on the Mississippi River across from Missouri, a former slave state, and it had German abolitionist residents. Founded before the Civil War, it was pro-Union during the war. A teacher from Evanston, Illinois, did extensive research on the Underground Railroad in Illinois and found a connection between Evanston, Springfield and Elsah.

The Riverview house. *Photograph by the author.*

According to the owner of this house, the basement has plenty of weird spaces that may have been Underground Railroad hiding places. She indicated that it is configured perfectly for this purpose. Many additions have been made over the years, and the construction of the Great River Road may have destroyed the tunnels that led to the river.

CHRISTIAN SERINI HOUSE, ELSAH, ILLINOIS (PRE–CIVIL WAR)

There is a space under the floor of the newer addition that was built on the back of the original house that is now used as an apartment. This space has a trapdoor in the floor that leads to a hiding place with rough-cut limestone walls and a dirt floor. The hidden room does not fit the

The Serini house. *Photograph by the author.*

footprint of the original building and could well have been used on the Underground Railroad. It could have been accessed by a secret door in the basement of the original building or through an entrance in the ground covered by an outbuilding.

One of my memorable Underground Railroad adventures occurred here. The lady who owned the business in the main portion of the building told me about the hiding place. She said a college student lived in the apartment and that I should knock on his door. Although I was a bit apprehensive, I did as she said. A wonderfully amiable and interested young man answered and invited me in. He opened the trapdoor and allowed me to photograph the room. He even said I was welcome to go down into it. Since I had just had knee surgery and would have needed a ladder, I reluctantly declined his courteous invitation.

Elsah was a regular stop on the route of sidewheel packet steamboats that ran daily between St. Louis, Alton and Keokuk. Napolean Mulliken of Alton was a part owner of the boats. The boiler tenders, deckhands, cooks and stewards were enslaved. Was this perhaps a cover for Underground Railroad activities?

GRAFTON, ILLINOIS

The *Pere Marquette State Park and Conservation Area* brochure (1967) noted that the "Underground Railroad was a well-kept secret of the [pre–Civil War] period in Grafton, Calhoun Point being the rendezvous for escaping slaves."

"THE MANSION," O'FALLON, ILLINOIS (1857)

This home was built by August Wastfield and served as an Underground Railroad safe house. Freedom seekers were hidden in three different places in the house, including under the stairs. The last five stairs to the cupola were removable. The house was located on the St. Louis–Vincennes stagecoach road. Abraham Lincoln purportedly stayed there.

COLLINSVILLE, ILLINOIS AND MARYVILLE, ILLINOIS REGION

Mary-Christine McMahon, a guide at the Glen Carbon Heritage Museum, explained that freedom seekers would have moved from Carbondale to Collinsville/Maryville to Alton. A farm in the eastern part of Collinsville was an Underground Railroad station, along with other farms in the area. The "Old Trading Post" (demolished) on Keebler Road in Maryville was a safe house. McMahon's great-great-uncle lived in Maryville, and his home was a station. He said that he left the barn and outbuilding doors open with food inside for freedom seekers. Hunters of enslaved people from Missouri went to the Old Trading Post and local stores for information on the freedom seekers. They would ask, for example, how much flour a family bought to see if it was an amount larger than that needed for a regular household.

McMahon also said that a preacher in Alton went across the Mississippi River to Missouri to preach, which was a cover for relaying Underground Railroad information.

OLD BETHEL BAPTIST CHURCH, CASEYVILLE, ILLINOIS

In 1809, James Lemen Sr. founded this abolitionist church that served as a stop on the Underground Railroad. A forty-by-sixty-foot frame building was constructed here in 1840. It had a trapdoor in the floor that led to a hiding place. The trapdoor was covered by a coal stove. Written records show that Black people were members of the church (the records list only their first names). Reverend James Mason Peck preached at the church's dedication ceremony. The congregation moved to a new building in 1977.

Obera Matthews related information on the Singleton family (free Black family, early family members were enslaved) of the Caseyville area in "Slave Escape Tale May Rescue Bethel Church" by Charles O. Stewart (*Metro-East Journal*, June 24, 1977) and a manuscript of *The Singleton Family Reunion* in the Collinsville Historical Museum archives. Matthews got this information from her aunt Alice Jones, who lived to be 102 years old. Matthews's grandfather James E. Singleton Sr.; his four brothers, Bertram, Leonard, Isaac and Oliver; his sister, Mary; and his cousin Ed accompanied Captain Lemen from Virginia to the Lemen Settlement in the Caseyville area of Illinois around 1845. Oliver organized the Underground Railroad system in the region, hiding freedom seekers in the Bethel Baptist Church. When pro-Southerners learned of Oliver's activities, his brother James put him in a wagon, covered him with vegetables and took him to the home of John Knowles, a safe house. Isaac's brothers and friends found him there and took him to "Cousin Martha's" in Alton. He was supposed to make his way to Canada but was never heard from again. The manuscript account says it was Isaac, not Oliver, who was the Underground Railroad conductor.

A statement of Isaac Singleton from the late nineteenth or early twentieth century is in the Bethel Baptist Church Archives and reads:

> *I was very actively involved with the Underground Railroad and helped to send many enslaved people, men, women and children, on to Alton, Illinois and from there to Canada and freedom. Locally, the Old Bethel Baptist Church in Caseyville was definitely a part of this main artery and a holdover in case of detection, and many a slave was hidden in the underground chamber that could be reached through a trapdoor in the main section of the church building.*

Kathleen Schultz Mendez's *Bethel Baptist Church of Caseyville: A Brief History, 1809–2009*, notes that church members' letters and family records indicate freedom seekers from St. Louis were hidden in the church on their way to Alton and Jacksonville. The church's meeting minutes from May 7, 1864, report that Brother Scott accused Brother Palmer of "helping fugitive slaves to obtain their freedom." Palmer admitted his guilt, and by a vote of 31–12, no action was taken against him.

One route used by conductors ran from Caseyville/Collinsville to the tunnels of the Edwardsville Brewery. The freedom seekers were then taken to the Three Mile House, north of Edwardsville, and on to Springfield.

EDWARDSVILLE BREWERY, EDWARDSVILLE, ILLINOIS (1858)

Henry Ritter and his brothers founded the Edwardsville Brewery in 1858 at the end of North Main Street. It had tunnels leading northeast to bricked caves in Cahokia Creek Bluff, near Indian Creek, where their beer was stored. The Ritters were active on the Underground Railroad.

Three Mile House, North of Edwardsville, Illinois (Circa 1858)

Tunnels led from the cellar to small, underground rooms in the backyard that were used as hiding places for freedom seekers. The house was a stop on the line that originated in Alton. It burned down in 1985, but some of the walls, rocks and gardens of nearby houses have incorporated bricks from it.

Charles Imboden House, Decatur, Illinois (1855)

There is a tunnel system under downtown Decatur, and many older buildings have entrances to the tunnels in their basements. Some houses that were built before the Civil War were equipped with double walls and passages in which to hide freedom seekers.

The Imboden house had a secret cellar and hidden passageway leading from the basement that were used on the Underground Railroad.

John Hossack House, Ottawa, Illinois (1854)

John Hossack was a successful businessman in lumber and grain. Like many other residents of the town, he was an abolitionist. His house served as an Underground Railroad station.

Congregational Church, Lyonsville, Illinois (1830s)

This church served as an Underground Railroad station during the Civil War. The Potawatomi, Ojibwe and Ottawa camped in the area in 1835 after signing the Treaty of Chicago, which forced them to relinquish their lands in northern Illinois and southern Wisconsin to the United States.

Green-Luther House, Plainfield, Illinois (Circa 1845)

This home was built by Dennison Green, who arrived in Plainfield in 1840. He was a member of the Baptist church and a devout abolitionist. According to oral tradition, his house was an Underground Railroad station, with the attic and cellar used as hiding places.

Pettengill House, Peoria, Illinois

Moses and Lucy Pettengill settled in Peoria in 1834. They lived in a house at the corner of Liberty and Jefferson Streets from 1836 to 1862. The home was demolished in 1910 and replaced by the Jefferson Hotel, which was, in turn, demolished to make way for the Peoria Civic Center. Moses and Lucy were Underground Railroad conductors and worked in conjunction with other conductors on both sides of the Illinois River. They were friends of Abraham Lincoln, and he stayed at their home when he was in town.

Lucy Pettengill led a group of local women who founded the Female Anti-Slavery Society of Peoria in 1843. In 1844, she helped establish the Female Anti-Slavery Society of Illinois.

Main Street Presbyterian Church, Peoria, Illinois

This church, known as the "Abolition Church," was founded by Moses and Lucy Pettengill. Moses was among those who met at the church in 1843 to form the Peoria Anti-Slavery Society (the meeting was broken up by a proslavery mob).

Geneseo, Illinois

In 1836, a group of Congregationalist families from Geneseo and Bergen, New York, settled in the area, founding the town of Geneseo, Illinois. They had signed a covenant vowing support for the antislavery cause and established the town specifically as an Underground Railroad hub. The Chicago, Rock Island and Pacific Railroad came through town in 1855 and was used in assisting freedom seekers.

Ann and George Richards were part of the second group of abolitionists who arrived in Geneseo, Illinois. They built a house that was an Underground Railroad station. Hiding holes for freedom seekers were built into the basement in 1855. Deacon Elisha Cone's cabin was also a safe house, with a hiding place in the attic.

The First Congregational Church was an Underground Railroad safe house beginning in the 1830s. The original church (1838) was a log building covered with canvas from a covered wagon. The cornerstone for the present church was laid in 1855.

Sheldon Peck Homestead, Lombard, Illinois (1839)

Sheldon Peck, a self-taught portrait painter and ardent abolitionist, formed an Underground Railroad network throughout Illinois, which probably included DuPage, Fox Valley, Whiteside County, Wheaton, Pekin, Rockford, Quincy, St. Louis and Sheboygan, Wisconsin. He had connections in each of these places. Peck's clapboard home hid freedom seekers through the 1850s. Many were hidden in the barn on the property. Peck held several antislavery meetings at his homestead and worked for the abolitionist newspaper the *Western Citizen*, which was published in Chicago. The homestead is now a museum open to the public and a site included in the National Park Service's National Underground Railroad Network to Freedom.

Owen Lovejoy Homestead, Princeton, Illinois (1838)

Lovejoy's home, an Underground Railroad safe house, contains hidden entrances to secret rooms. Owen was Elijah's brother. Much has been written about Owen that is easily accessible on the internet. The house is open seasonally to the public for tours. The Bryants were also Underground Railroad conductors in Princeton.

JOHN JONES'S SHOP, CHICAGO, ILLINOIS

Jones was the leader of a free Black community in Chicago and an Underground Railroad conductor. Robert McCormick and Joseph Medill, founders of the *Daily Tribune* newspaper, were abolitionists and provided printing services to Jones for an antislavery pamphlet. From his shop on Dearborn Street, Jones placed freedom seekers on Great Lakes steamers to Detroit. They were then hidden at the Second Baptist Church there by the Colored Vigilant Committee, which was led by George DeBaptiste. The committee was a group of free Black people, mostly from Kentucky, who helped freedom seekers get from Detroit to Canada.

There are dozens of Underground Railroad sites in suburban Chicago, including the Quinn Chapel African Methodist Episcopal Church. Wheaton College (Blanchard Hall) and the town of Wheaton, close to Chicago, were also involved in the Underground Railroad. A house at Forty-Seventh and Racine Streets in the Chicago suburb of Englewood was, per oral tradition, a station on the Underground Railroad.

Reverend Richard De Baptiste was an Underground Railroad conductor and pastor of the Olivette Baptist Church in the Bronzeville area of Chicago. His brother George had a boat that transported freedom seekers from Detroit to Canada under cover of darkness.

John and Aggie Ton lived in what is now South Holland, a suburb of Chicago. They were Dutch farmers and Underground Railroad conductors, along with the Cuyper family, also Dutch farmers. They helped freedom seekers get to Detroit.

GRAUE MILL AND MUSEUM, OAK BROOK, ILLINOIS (1849)

The mill's owner, Frederick Graue, hid freedom seekers in the basement of the gristmill on Salt Creek. Both Black and white agents brought food to them. The mill and museum are open to the public seasonally for tours.

ISRAEL AND AVIS BLODGETT HOUSE, DOWNER'S GROVE, ILLINOIS

The Blodgetts, who lived in this house from 1840 to 1861, transported freedom seekers from this home to Philo Carpenter's house in Chicago. Their activities are documented through firsthand accounts of three of the Blodgetts children. In the 1840s and 1850s, Israel was a member, along with other local Underground Railroad conductors, of the Liberty and Free Democracy Parties. He and Avis were members of the First Congregational Church in Naperville, Illinois. The site is on the National Park Service's National Underground Railroad Network to Freedom (2023).

AFRICA/LOCUST GROVE, ILLINOIS

This was a free Black and freedom seeker settlement in the northeast corner of Williamson County. Involved in Underground Railroad activities, it was founded by servants whose indentures had expired and free Black people.

NEW PHILADELPHIA, ILLINOIS (1836)

This free Black community was founded in 1836 by Frank McWorter, a free Black man. It served as a safe haven for freedom seekers. It was the first town in the United States platted and registered by a Black person before the Civil War. McWorter was a formerly enslaved man who saved up enough money to buy the freedom of his wife, himself and thirteen family members. New Philadelphia is now a National Historic Landmark.

PIN OAK, ILLINOIS (CIRCA 1817/1818)

This settlement was founded by twenty-two free Black people and harbored freedom seekers. It is in the vicinity of Edwardsville. In the 1830s, over three hundred free Black people were residing in Pin Oak. Former freedom seeker Harry Dougherty, freed in 1865, owned land in Pin Oak.

BROOKLYN, ILLINOIS (CIRCA 1829)

Brooklyn was founded around 1829, when Priscilla "Mother" Baltimore, an enslaved woman who bought her own freedom, led eleven families of free Black people and freedom seekers from St. Louis across the Mississippi River to Illinois, where they established a freedom village in the American Bottoms. Along with William Paul Quinn, a missionary of the African Methodist Episcopal church, she established Brooklyn African Methodist Episcopal Church in 1836 (which burned down in the 1870s and was rebuilt at same location; it is now known as Quinn Chapel African Methodist Episcopal Church). Baltimore and the congregation worked on the Underground Railroad, assisting freedom seekers. They worked in conjunction with nearby Antioch Baptist Church (1838). Freedom seekers hid in a cellar underneath Quinn Chapel and were then sent into the woods to move on to Alton, Illinois. The current Quinn Chapel was built in the 1870s. Baltimore was buried in Bellefontaine Cemetery in St. Louis.

Left: Quinn Chapel AME Church. *Photograph by the author.*

Right: Antioch Baptist Church. *Photograph by the author.*

Lakeview/Pond Settlement, Illinois (Early Nineteenth Century)

This settlement was founded by free Black people in Saline County shortly after the War of 1812 and was active on the Underground Railroad. Its residents assisted freedom seekers from the salt springs and the Old Slave House in southern Illinois.

Other Pre–Civil War African American Settlements in Illinois

Pinkstaff was established by free Black people around 1812, and Nigger Hill/Grayson was founded in the 1820s. Nigger Spring was started by former enslaved people who worked at the salt springs and purchased their freedom. South America had a post office by 1853, and Nigger Settlement/Higginbotham was settled by free Black people in the 1820s. A Black community developed in Allen in the 1830s; it was friendly with the Quakers in nearby Johnson County. An unnamed settlement was founded in 1830 by Joseph Ivey. By 1835, thirty-five free Black people and some white people lived there. It was relocated to another location by 1840.

These free Black communities assisted freedom seekers by helping them move to the next station or by incorporating them into their own social circles.

PART II

BURIAL SITES OF ENSLAVED PEOPLE IN MISSOURI

God's time is always near. He gave me my strength and he set the North Star in the heavens. He meant I should be free.

—*Harriet Tubman*

5

OVERVIEW

Some of the enslaved people of Missouri were buried in large, well-known cemeteries; some were buried in smaller church graveyards; some were buried in private family cemeteries; and some are buried in cemeteries set aside for the enslaved. Almost all of them were buried in unmarked graves. In some instances, a grave may have been marked by yucca plants or Mason jars. Quinette Cemetery is still graced with old yucca plants, and Mason jars were found not too long ago at Mt. Pleasant Colored Baptist Church Cemetery (see the following section).

The burials of enslaved people have been documented in the records of Bellefontaine Cemetery, Calvary Cemetery, Oak Hill Cemetery, Rock Hill Presbyterian Church Cemetery and Old Des Peres Presbyterian Church Cemetery, all in St. Louis County.[††] There are three Black commercial cemeteries in St. Louis: Greenwood Cemetery (1874), Father Dickson Cemetery (1903) and Washington Park Cemetery (1920).

Per Morris, in the late nineteenth century, trustees may have acted on behalf of a small church to purchase donated land (usually one to two acres) for use as a Black cemetery per a deed stipulation. Examples of this include Ebenezer Cemetery (Pacific), Hope Cemetery (Pacific), Sage Chapel Cemetery (O'Fallon), Quinette Cemetery, Union Baptist Cemetery, First Baptist Church of Chesterfield Cemetery, Ballwin African American Cemetery and New Coldwater Burying Ground in St. Louis County.

---

†† Morris, *Sacred Greenspace*.

6

SITES

Old Des Peres Presbyterian Church Cemetery, Frontenac, St. Louis County, Missouri (1833)

The burial site of enslaved people was unmarked until 1983, when a boulder with a metal plaque was placed there. It is located in the southeast corner of the cemetery. The original land donors stipulated that the congregation set aside a cemetery with a section designated for the burial of their enslaved people. Information on the church can be found in chapter 2 of this book.

Father Dickson Cemetery, Crestwood, St. Louis County, Missouri (1903)

This was one of the first Black public cemeteries in St. Louis. It was named for Reverend Moses Dickson, a Black abolitionist leader who was born free in Ohio in 1824. In 1846, he founded the Knights of Liberty and Order of Twelve, secret organizations that enlisted and armed enslaved persons for rebellion. He was later ordained as an African Methodist Episcopal minister. Dickson devoted himself to social activism on behalf of Black people and cofounded the Lincoln Institute (now Lincoln University) in Jefferson City.

Above: Old Des Peres Presbyterian Church's signage. *Photograph by the author.*

Left: The burial site of the enslaved at Old Des Presbyterian Church's cemetery. *Photograph by the author.*

He was also president of the Refugee Relief Board, which helped relocate around sixteen thousand formerly enslaved people. The National Park Service's website says Father Dickson was "a member of the Underground Railroad and community leader during the Civil War era." *Sappington-Concord: A History* (1999) says that he "arrived in St. Louis and became one of the organizers of the Underground Railroad."

James Milton Turner and John Vashon were also buried here. Turner was born into slavery, purchased by his father and secretly sent to school. He was a cofounder of Lincoln University and the first Black United States ambassador to Liberia. Vashon was a well-known lawyer and teacher. He was the son of Black abolitionists George and Susan Vashon.

There are four Mary Balls listed as being buried here. One was born into slavery in 1852 in Kentucky. She was petitioned for freedom as a child, with her value listed as $1,000. She was eventually freed by law and came to St. Louis, where she worked as a cook. She was killed at the age of sixty-four by a coal fire explosion. The children and grandchildren of enslaved people were buried here, including Wattie Brown, James Boyd and Henry "Steamboat" Lewis. Jasper Pettit, born enslaved in 1844 in Wayne County, Missouri, was also buried in Father Dickson Cemetery. His parents were enslaved by Dr. Pettit. An 1850 slave inventory shows he enslaved eighteen people, six of them young children, most likely including Jasper. Jasper was a member of the United States Colored Troops Heavy Artillery at the end of the Civil War.

Pauline Hayden Salmon was born in the West Indies. She was probably enslaved and brought to St. Louis. Susan Vashon cared for wounded soldiers and Black refugees during the Civil War. Madam C.J. Walker, a famous Black businesswoman whose parents were enslaved, was buried in New York City but has a cenotaph at Father Dickson Cemetery.

The Ward family plot is marked with simple concrete blocks with etched metal plates tarred in place. No dates or names remain. It is likely that there are unmarked graves of formerly enslaved people in the cemetery.

More than six thousand Black people were buried in Father Dickson Cemetery, including veterans of the Civil War, Spanish-American War, World War I, World War II and the Korean War.

HANLEY HOUSE, CLAYTON, ST. LOUIS COUNTY, MISSOURI (1855)

This house was built by Martin Hanley, an enslaver. According to a docent, there is an unmarked burial site for enslaved people on the property.

QUINETTE CEMETERY, KIRKWOOD, ST. LOUIS COUNTY, MISSOURI (CIRCA THE MID-NINETEENTH CENTURY)

This is the burial place of one hundred to two hundred people. It is possible that freedom seekers who died while moving on the Underground Railroad through Kirkwood and Webster Groves were buried here. Four United States Colored Troops soldiers were also buried here. A tiny headstone marked "J.B." may indicate the now sunken grave of an enslaved person who was buried in his enslaver's family plot (or it may be a footstone). A couple of plot cornerstones remain today.

The property was originally owned by the federal government and used as a cemetery for prisoners of war during the Civil War. In 1866, it was privately owned, and in 1873, it was transferred to the trustees of Olive Chapel African Methodist Episcopal Church. Beginning in 1866, it offered free burials to Black people who lived within a five-mile radius of the church and those who received approval from the church's trustees.

Enslaved people, Black military veterans and Kirkwood founders were all buried here. Many burials took place without coffins or with the bodies placed in simple pine boxes. Markers were often limestone slabs, and graves were decorated with yucca plants, flowers, Mason jars and shells. Many of the graves were unmarked.

FIRST BAPTIST CHURCH OF CHESTERFIELD CEMETERY, CHESTERFIELD, ST. LOUIS COUNTY, MISSOURI (1846)

In 1846, enslaver Maria Long granted her enslaved people a plot of land where they could build their own church. Half of the lot was reserved for a church, and the other half was left for a cemetery. The original church/school building was a crude log cabin. In 1870, a larger log building was constructed. In 1875, the Longs legally transferred the land to the formerly enslaved people, and the church was chartered that same year. The cemetery contains the graves of enslaved and formerly enslaved people and their descendants.

GREENWOOD CEMETERY, HILLSDALE, ST. LOUIS COUNTY, MISSOURI (1874)

This thirty-acre cemetery contains the graves of thirty thousand Black people, including those of an aid to Abraham Lincoln, a civil rights leader (Charlton Tandy), Civil War veterans, buffalo soldiers, blues and jazz musicians and American folk figure Lee Shelton of "Stagger Lee" fame. It was the region's first commercial cemetery for Black Americans. Around five thousand people who were born during the era of slavery were buried here.

Harriet Scott's memorial in Greenwood Cemetery. *Photograph by the author.*

Harriet Scott, Dred Scott's wife, was buried here. A modern monument is in the area of her grave now. Her actual grave site is located to the north of the memorial. The Professional Tour Guides Association of St. Louis and Dorris Keeven Franke are working to get a marker placed on the site. Harriet has a cenotaph next to Dred's marker in Calvary Cemetery in St. Louis County.

Lucy Ann Delaney, an author and activist, was emancipated via a freedom suit in the 1840s and was buried at Greenwood Cemetery. She wrote the slave narrative *From the Darkness Cometh the Light, or, Struggles for Freedom*, the only first-person account of a freedom suit, published in 1891.

Other enslaved people buried at Greenwood Cemetery include Nancy, who was given as a gift to a bride to be used as her personal worker. Nancy's mother was also enslaved. Nancy eventually escaped to Canada. Gus Turner was born into slavery in Alabama and has no headstone. Washington Reed was a sergeant in the Union army during the Civil War and later purchased land in what is now Breckenridge Hills.

ROCK HILL PRESBYTERIAN CHURCH CEMETERY, ROCK HILL, ST. LOUIS COUNTY, MISSOURI (CHURCH, CIRCA 1845)

In 1845, James Marshall founded this church in Rock Hill. Oral tradition says that the roof was built by enslaved people on a Sunday as their

Rock Hill
Presbyterian Church.
Missouri Preservation,
www.preservemo.org.

contribution to the church. Black and white people worshipped together in the building, but the enslaved were confined to a second-story balcony, or "slave gallery." Old Bonhomme Presbyterian Church also has an extant balcony where enslaved people were forced to sit.

Originally, there was a church cemetery where both Black and white people were buried. Most of the bodies were moved to Oak Hill Cemetery in 1866 and later on. The church was demolished not too long ago to make way for a gas station. The stones were supposedly saved and moved to a winery in St. Charles, where the owners hope to eventually rebuild the structure. The historic Fairfax house still stands next to the gas station.

Lost Cemetery, Fee Fee Road, near Natural Bridge, Bridgeton, St. Louis County, Missouri

This cemetery was located near the historic Payne-Gentry house, which is still standing. According to local historian and tour guide Jeanne Keirle, it contained the burial sites of enslaved people. I believe it was most likely destroyed for the airport's expansion.

Conway Family Cemetery, Chesterfield, St. Louis County, Missouri

This cemetery is located on the south side of Conway Road, west of Highway 141. It includes an enslaved burial area, which was immediately west of the family home (later demolished, but foundation stones are still visible in the bushes). Originally, the enslaved burial section and family burial section were separated by a line of cedar trees. The cemetery contains about thirty graves, including those of the enslaved people.

The Conway family donated the land for Old Bonhomme Presbyterian Church across

The marker for the burial site of the enslaved at Conway Family Cemetery. *Photograph by the author.*

the street and just east of the cemetery in 1816. They came to Chesterfield from England in 1797. Joseph Conway, a Revolutionary War soldier, was buried here. The cemetery's burials date from 1801 to 1957. A later marker memorializes the burial area of the enslaved.

FEE FEE (CREEK) BAPTIST CHURCH (1829) AND CEMETERY (1822), BRIDGETON, ST. LOUIS COUNTY, MISSOURI

Illinois pastor Thomas Musick moved to Florissant and, with several other families, established a Baptist congregation on the banks of Fee Fee Creek in 1807. The current church building was constructed in 1829, and the church's cemetery was plotted in 1822. The remains of early French settlers of St. Louis were moved from the St. Louis City burial ground to a common grave in the corner of this cemetery around 1814. The cemetery contains many scattered and unmarked graves, some probably belonging to the people who were enslaved by early settlers. A local Civil War Confederate soldier, John Morgan Utz, who was executed for spying, was also buried here.

Old Fee Fee Baptist Church. *Photograph by the author.*

MT. OLIVE CEMETERY OF LEMAY, ST. LOUIS COUNTY, MISSOURI (1849)

This cemetery was established for the burials of victims of the 1849 cholera epidemic. It contains a pre–Civil War tombstone for a "colored servant," which was the antebellum terminology used for an enslaved person. A marker was placed for Dick, an enslaved man who died in the epidemic. The marker was placed by his enslaver.

The original Mount Olive Cemetery was opened in 1823 as the first parish burial ground for St. Mary and Joseph Catholic Church in Carondelet. By 1839, the cemetery was full, and it was closed. The northern portion of the 1849 cemetery was reserved for Catholics, and the southern portion was used for Protestants. Archbishop Kendrick named the northern portion Mt. Olive Cemetery, after the original cemetery.

COLD WATER (CREEK) CEMETERY, FLORISSANT, ST. LOUIS COUNTY, MISSOURI (CIRCA 1808)

Oral tradition says that an eight-cornered Methodist church built in the form of a cross was established here around 1808, and it had a graveyard on its grounds. Gina Seibe of Historic Florissant Inc. noted that the enslaved people of Musick, Carrico and Patterson were buried in the family plots in unmarked graves.

NEW COLDWATER BURIAL GROUNDS, FLORISSANT, ST. LOUIS COUNTY, MISSOURI (1886)

Delia Hayes and Henry Vincent, formerly enslaved people, established this cemetery and were buried in it.

Family Cemeteries of Early Enslavers, Florissant, Missouri Area

Some early landowners in the Florissant area were enslavers: Musick, Patterson, Hyatt, Hume, Shackelford and Richardson. The enslaved people of the Hyatts had their own church and graveyard located on Shackelford Road, about a mile south of New Halls Ferry Road. The enslaved people of the Pattersons had a church and graveyard near Cold Water Creek and Old Halls Ferry Road, two miles west of Black Jack. The Shackelford farm on the south side of New Halls Ferry Road, east of Shackelford Road, contains a plot were enslaved people were buried. Those who were enslaved by the Humes were buried at the Hume farm on Shackelford and Patterson Roads, near Florissant.

Calvary Cemetery, St. Louis

Dred Scott, the subject of the famous freedom suit that went all the way to the United States Supreme Court, was buried here. His wife, Harriet, has a cenotaph here. She was buried in Greenwood Cemetery. Union Civil War general William Tecumseh Sherman was buried nearby. It is common for people to leave pennies at Dred's grave, an ancient tradition.

Pelagie, an enslaved woman who married Mr. Rutger, was buried in Cavalry Cemetery. She inherited most of the land in what is now Lafayette Park. She donated the funds to build the bell tower in the Rutger plot. The bell rang every day, and Pelagie came by carriage from Lafayette Park to visit the plot daily.

The Mullanphys were enslavers. The small, arched marker of a woman enslaved by the family, Angelina Smith-Liny, sits next to the marker of the Mullanphys' grandson John Mullanphy Chambers. Her marker is inscribed, "Angelina Smith-Liny / A Colored Slave / Kind and Loyal / 1827–1915."

Enslaved people were buried in unmarked graves in their enslavers' plots throughout the cemetery. An area called "the meadow" contains the marked graves of some of St. Louis's founding families. Thousands of mixed bones have been found there, including those of enslaved people. Bodies were moved here from the old city cemeteries. The Chouteau plots in the cemetery almost certainly contain the unmarked graves of the enslaved. Madame Marie Terese Bourgeois Chouteau, an enslaver and the city's matriarch, was buried in Pierre Chouteau's plot, although no one knows exactly where.

In the "Old Priest's Lot," Natives and Spanish soldiers were buried beneath a wooden cross, long ago lost to history. It is not known exactly where this cross was located. Spanish soldiers and their enslaved people, initially buried at Fort Bellefontaine, were moved to this spot.

The cemetery contains a memorial commemorating the first six enslaved people the Jesuits brought from Maryland in 1823 to establish St. Stanislaus Seminary in Florissant. They are named later in this book. The monument is inscribed, "Their labor, not freely given, helped to establish a Jesuit presence in the Midwest."

JEFFERSON BARRACKS NATIONAL CEMETERY, ST. LOUIS COUNTY, MISSOURI

This cemetery contains a memorial dedicated to 175 soldiers of the Fifty-Sixth United States Colored Infantry. The obelisk monument was placed in the late 1860s. These soldiers, noncommissioned officers and enlisted men, died of cholera in 1866 and were interred at Jefferson Barracks in 1939.

MUSICK BAPTIST CHURCH AND CEMETERY, MARYLAND HEIGHTS, ST. LOUIS COUNTY, MISSOURI

Per oral tradition, Thomas Musick, a pastor from Illinois, heard his enslaved people singing spirituals in his barn in 1811. This inspired him to give them land to build a church. The first church was a log cabin, which eventually evolved into the two-story wooden structure that stands there today. It has stood in the same location for over two hundred years. The church's cemetery contains scattered graves, most of them unmarked, undoubtedly containing many remains of enslaved people.

SAPPINGTON FAMILY CEMETERY, CRESTWOOD, ST. LOUIS COUNTY, MISSOURI (1811)

This cemetery is located on Watson Road, east of Sappington Road. Thomas Sappington enslaved eleven people. His house on Sappington Road was built by them. *Sappington-Concord: A History* notes that "a section was provided for the burial of Negroes." They were buried in unmarked graves.

BELLEFONTAINE CEMETERY, ST. LOUIS, MISSOURI (1849)

Note: The information in this section was provided by Dan Fuller of Bellefontaine Cemetery.

One of the top historic garden cemeteries in the United States, this nonsectarian cemetery has an abundance of Black American history. The graves of Jewish people and people of color were not segregated, as they were in many other cemeteries of the period (the cemetery did struggle against regulations prohibiting the burial of free people of color from 1854 to 1874).

The Roberson brothers, free Black barbers who worked at the Barnum Hotel, were buried here. William and Francis "Frank" Roberson became two of the wealthiest Black people in St. Louis while working as barbers before the Civil War. William and Frank formed the F. Roberson and Brothers Company. Frank's shop was located under the Barnum Hotel at Second and Walnut Streets. He had moved to St. Louis from Virginia in 1848 and first had a shop at 106 North Third Street. By 1857, he had opened the shop in the Barnum Hotel with his brother William. A third brother, Robert, joined the business later on. William Roberson married Lucy Jefferson, a woman enslaved by Thomas Jefferson who was also related to him (DNA proved the relationship, but the DNA of Lucy's father, Robert, is needed to prove a direct descendancy). William helped establish the Prince Hall Masons in Missouri in the 1850s.

Enslaved people were buried in unmarked areas in family plots throughout the cemetery. A few bought their own plots, but most plots belonged to the enslavers, who requested that their enslaved be buried in the family plot.

There is an unmarked Black lot across from the Schloeman monument. It is an empty area in front of the Smith monument that contains a family lot (no. 3978) with thirteen burials but not a single stone. The people buried

Above: The Robersons' grave at Bellefontaine Cemetery. *Photograph by the author.*

Left: John Anderson's grave at Bellefontaine Cemetery. *Photograph by the author.*

there were associated with the education of Black people. Susan Vashon was originally buried in Bellefontaine Cemetery, but her remains were later moved to Father Dickson Cemetery.

Luther Martin Kennett was the mayor of St. Louis from 1850 to 1853. He has a huge burial plot with corner markers. There are four small markers located away from the main monument. One is for Alfred Alexander, a man who was enslaved by the Kennett family. He may have been Aunt Nelly Warren's helper (see the following section).

Free Black people, including John Berry Meachum (see the previous section of this book), John Richard Anderson and Emanuel Cartwright, were buried in the Baptist preachers' lot. Meachum's wife, Mary, has a cenotaph on John's monument. It is not known where she was buried. Reverend Anderson founded Second (Central) Baptist Church and reportedly assisted Elijah Lovejoy with the printing of abolitionist pamphlets at the time Lovejoy was killed by a mob in Alton, Illinois. Reverend Anderson died in 1863, and 150 carriages took part in his funeral procession.

Grace Montague was a nurse for the Williamses' children and was buried in the family plot. She may have been enslaved and later freed by Thornton Grimsley, the father of the woman who married Henry T. Blow (related to the Dred Scott case). Grace was buried with the children she cared for.

"Aunt Nelly" Warren was an enslaved nanny of the George Collier family. She died in 1857. She was buried in the family plot at their request. The main Collier monument contains a marker for her. She also has her own headstone next to that of a Collier son, within the circular path of headstones around the main monument. Both markers contain the word "colored." It was quite unusual for an enslaved person to have a marker, much less two. The Collier family must have been fond of Aunt Nelly. George Collier was an enslaver. His wife was a Portage des Sioux Saucier and one of the richest women in St. Louis. His mother, Catherine Collier of St. Charles, educated Black students at Collier's Cottage.

Priscilla Baltimore (see the previous section of this book) was buried in Bellefontaine Cemetery. Her marker was placed at a later date (in 2008). The area around her grave contains unmarked graves, possibly those of free Black people. The marker next to hers is that of a free Black woman who died in her teens. Both were buried in a public lot, where one grave at a time could be purchased.

Underground Railroad conductor Artemus Bullard was buried here (see the previous section of this book). The cemetery also contains the grave of

The Warren family's grave at Bellefontaine Cemetery. *Photograph by the author.*

Colonel Robert Quarles, who impregnated Caroline Quarlls's (her name was spelled this way by her family; it is spelled "Quarles" on Robert's grave) mother, one of the women he enslaved.

William Clark, the coleader of the famous Lewis and Clark Expedition, has a plot that contains two headstones for Black people. Lewis Wilson's marker says: "A faithful retainer of the family." Emmeline Payne's reads: "A good and faithful servant." While they were called "retainer" and "servant," they were most likely enslaved and may have been enslaved by Clark or one of his descendants. They are both listed as "colored" in the cemetery's records. York, an enslaved man who accompanied the Lewis and Clark Expedition, asked Clark for his freedom when they returned home, and Clark beat him for simply asking. Several years later, one of Clark's friends talked him into freeing York. York established a wagon-making business in Louisville, Kentucky. After that, he was lost to history.

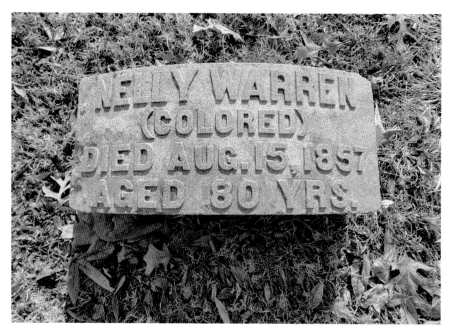

Nelly Warren's grave at Bellefontaine Cemetery. *Photograph by the author.*

Priscilla Baltimore's grave at Bellefontaine Cemetery. *Photograph by the author.*

Henry Lewis was a servant of Peter Lindell, whose will stipulated Lewis should be buried in the Lindell family plot. He was buried as close to Lindell as possible.

Susan Rutherford, a "nurse," was buried in 1901 without a marker. A later marker has the following inscribed on it: "Faithful Unto Death." It is not known whether she was enslaved.

Workers for the Carter family Harry Hurst (1780–1860), Priscilla Hurst (1813–1893) and Millie Strother were buried in the Carter family lot. It is unknown whether they were enslaved. All three of their names are listed on one stone in a corner of the lot.

James Good was buried next to the family mausoleum in the Goodfellow plot. He was enslaved by the family and worked for them after emancipation. He could not hear or talk and died in a fire at the Goodfellow estate in O'Fallon while trying to save the contents of the house. He had already saved the children.

SECOND CATHOLIC BURYING GROUND, ST. LOUIS CITY, MISSOURI (1823)

This burial ground was located at Dr. Martin Luther King Drive and Jefferson Avenue. The land for the cemetery, part of William Stokes's farm, was donated by him in 1823. According to historical research and osteological analysis, Creole people, free and enslaved Black people and Natives were buried there.

ST. LOUIS CITY CEMETERIES

The City of St. Louis had four cemeteries in its early days. Some of the burials there were those of free and enslaved Black people. When the cemeteries became full, some bodies were moved to other cemeteries. One of these cemeteries was located on the site of what is now Benton Park. These burial grounds are now lost to history.

St. Peter's Cemetery, St. Louis City, Missouri (1840s)

This cemetery on Lucas and Hunt Roads was founded in the 1840s by Germans. It has an area that contains hundreds of unmarked graves, with remains buried two and three deep. This area contains the graves of Archer and Julia Alexander (see the previous section in this book). The plot in which they were buried is known, but we do not know exactly where in the plot they were buried.

First Wesleyan Cemetery, St. Louis City, Missouri

This cemetery was located near Grand and Laclede Avenues. Dred Scott was initially buried here, but his remains were later moved to Calvary Cemetery. First Wesleyan Cemetery had sections for Black people and contains the grave sites of enslaved and free Black people.

Old St. Ferdinand Cemetery/Spanish Land Grant Park, Florissant, St. Louis County, Missouri (Circa 1790)

Joseph Robidoux III was a fur trader in Florissant and established a fur trading post in Blacksnake Hills (St. Joseph), Missouri, in 1827. According to Rosemary Davison in *Florissant, Missouri,* several of his enslaved people were buried in Old St. Ferdinand Cemetery.

New St. Ferdinand Cemetery, Florissant, St. Louis County, Missouri (1876)

According to Gina Seibe of Historic Florissant Inc., remains were moved here from Old St. Ferdinand Cemetery. The Queen family lot in the southwest section of New St. Ferdinand Cemetery contains the unmarked graves of enslaved people. The first row of this section contains about five lots owned by St. Stanislaus Seminary, where their enslaved, not the priests, were buried. According to Andrew Theising in *In the Walnut Grove: A Consideration of the People Enslaved in & Around Florissant, Missouri*, the formerly enslaved who were buried there include Rose Duke, enslaved by Mrs. Chambers, and James O'Brien, enslaved by the Jesuits at St. Stanislaus Seminary.

Burial Site of Sappington Family Enslaved, St. Louis County, Missouri

Now lost, this burial site was located behind the barns of Jack and Thomas Jefferson Sappington's farms. The location would now be on the Westminster Estates and Lindbergh High School properties.

Jefferson Barracks National Cemetery, St. Louis County, Missouri

The remains of some of the freed men in the Fifty-Sixth United States Colored Infantry were relocated to a mass grave here in 1939.

"Old Slave Cemetery" (Coleman Slave Cemetery), Wildwood, Missouri

This burial ground contains more than sixty uninscribed rough limestone markers that denote the grave sites of people who were enslaved by the Colemans. The markers were gathered and placed by them. It was professionally surveyed in January 2013, and each slab was marked with a flag. The cemetery was most likely used by the people enslaved by Reverend Robert Coleman and his sons before the Civil War and possibly for a short time afterward. The unnamed creek running along its edge has flooded many times and eroded the burial ground. Some markers are now buried, but fortunately, no remains have surfaced.

William Coleman inherited the cemetery. A portion of the land containing the cemetery was owned by William Coleman's descendants until at least 1940, and all of them farmed the land.

Sally Branson, who lived across the street from the cemetery for many years, indicated there was one marked stone. It had the name "Harris" hand chiseled into the limestone. Could this have been the grave of the Black overseer? Unfortunately, this marker was stolen in the 1980s.

Mt. Pleasant Colored Baptist Church and Cemetery, Wildwood, Missouri (Circa 1841)

This church was given to freed people by the church trustees in 1871–72. The burials of Black people began here circa 1880. Mason jars, which were typically used to mark the graves of Black people, were found in this cemetery. A depression on the slope of a hill denotes a grave that has sunken due to erosion. A pond where the Tylers baptized family members was located below the burial ground. The church burned down in 1950, and all that remain are portions of its foundation and a front step.

Several of the people enslaved by the Colemans and Tylers were members of the United States Colored Troops (USCT) during the Civil War. It is unclear how these particular enslaved persons become USCT soldiers. Some of them were buried in the Mount Pleasant Colored Baptist Church Cemetery, including Henry Hicks, Company F, USCT, a possible runaway; Louis Rollins, Company F, USCT, a possible runaway who was enslaved by James Pleasance, part of the Colemans' extended family; and Elijah Madison, Company F, USCT.

Elijah Madison was born into slavery in 1841 on the Coleman plantation. It is documented that he was enslaved by Robert Coleman. He enlisted in the Union army in 1864 in Melrose, Missouri, a German area, and then went to Benton Barracks in St. Louis, where he spent five weeks battling with pneumonia. He was discharged as a corporal in 1866 and returned to Wildwood. Madison married Elizabeth West and became a successful farmer. They had fifteen children. Later in life, Madison moved to Elmwood, Missouri, and became a minister. He died in 1922. Antioch Baptist Church has the original records documenting the baptisms of many enslaved people in the area, including that of Madison.

Bertha Rollins (1848–1924), the wife of Louis who was enslaved by the Colemans' extended family; Carrie and George Brown, born enslaved by the Colemans; James Green, whose parents were enslaved; and Elijah Madison's brother Stapleton, along with his wife and daughter, were also buried in Mount Pleasant Colored Baptist Church Cemetery.

Rock Bethel Methodist Church, Wildwood, Missouri (Dedicated 1859)

This church initially had a German congregation. It served as a dividing line of sorts between the Germans and "Brits," or planters, from Virginia. The church building, made of limestone and wood, still has its original large wooden door. The back wooden wall is almost gone now. The congregation moved, and the church and its cemetery are now in Pond, Missouri (see the Bethel Church Cemetery's section). There are about one hundred unmarked graves of enslaved people behind the cemetery at the tree line.

Union Baptist Church and African Baptist Burying Ground, Westland Acres, Missouri

The history of this church dates to the Colored African Church and Antioch Baptist Church. Much of what we know about it comes from oral tradition provided by Maggie Wash Frazier. The people who were enslaved by the Longs, Stevens and Colemans were involved in this church's long history. In 1865, two free Black people bought land from their former enslaver and then sold one acre for the site of the Colored African Baptist Church. Its membership formed the core of the future Union Baptist Church. A log cabin on a hill was the church in winter and school in summer. Most church members were from the West family. William West was enslaved by the Longs and eventually freed. He donated land for the first church. The Wests and Fraziers were buried in the cemetery. The cemetery contains some uninscribed, rough stones, most likely grave markers. One might denote William West's grave site. The current Union Baptist Church was built later.

ANTIOCH BAPTIST CHURCH, WILDWOOD, MISSOURI

This church was established in 1841 by families from Virginia. The Colemans were members. The congregation from Mount Pleasant moved here. Before the Civil War, both white and Black enslaved people worshipped at the church, but after the war, only white men were allowed to govern it. The church relocated in 1860, and a new stucco structure encased the old building in 1921.

BETHEL CHURCH & CEMETERY, WILDWOOD, MISSOURI

This church began as Rock Bethel Methodist Church (see previous section). Although the church building was finished in 1875, some graves date to the 1850s and 1860s. According to oral history, enslaved people were buried at the back of the cemetery, near the tree line, in an unmarked area.

LORIMORE ESTATE, WILDWOOD, MISSOURI

Enslaved people were buried here on a hill overlooking the river bluffs. A log cabin is still on the site.

RICHARDSON CEMETERY, ARNOLD, MISSOURI (1841/1867)

The first burial here took place in 1841, and the land was officially designated a burial ground in 1867. John Richardson bought two hundred acres for $200, and the cemetery was laid out in two sections: the north for the Richardson family and the south for the Hunt family. Veterans of the War of 1812, Mexican War and Civil War (Confederate and Union) were buried here, along with direct descendants of French settlers who lived in St. Louis in 1767 (Gamache). Several families in the area were enslavers; the 1850 slave census names them as the Whites, Cadwalladers, Stines, Pipkins, Waterses, Richardsons, Gregoris/Gregorys and Frederitzis. Oral tradition from the Frederitzi family indicates that three people who were enslaved or formerly enslaved by Peter Frederitzi were buried just outside of section R, along the northern rock border. Napolean Bonaparte Franklin, who moved to the area from the Carolinas, enslaved nine people in 1840 and four people in 1850 in Rock Township.

McROBERTS FAMILY CEMETERY AND SCOTT FAMILY CEMETERY, ST. CHARLES COUNTY, MISSOURI

According to local cemetery researcher Mazie Dalton, these recently discovered cemeteries contain some uninscribed limestone markers. Death certificates date to 1866, but there are most likely older burial sites here. Forty-two enslaved people were buried in the two cemeteries. A small Black community was located nearby for several decades.

The McRoberts Cemetery is a Black family cemetery. Henderson McRoberts was an enslaved man who served in the United States Colored Troops in the Civil War. His enslaver was probably Preston McRoberts.

The rough limestone marker of the enslaved with yucca plants at McRoberts and Scott Cemeteries. *Photograph by Mazie Dalton, used with permission.*

St. Charles Borromeo Church Cemetery, St. Charles, Missouri

There are records of burials of enslaved, mixed race and Black people in the old cemetery. Of the one hundred deaths recorded between 1797 and 1866, thirty-one were Natives, nine were biracial people, sixteen were people who were "not enslaved of anyone" and forty-four were "negro" enslaved. One record reads: "N. [Negro], Peter, ca. 100 years (slave), 1862."

Oak Grove Cemetery, St. Charles, Missouri (1860)

According to the sexton's records, this cemetery's potter's field contains the burial sites of enslaved people. A person who was enslaved by the Redman family was buried in an unmarked grave in the family's plot.

Black Walnut Cemetery, Black Walnut, St. Charles County, Missouri (1810)

This cemetery contains the grave of Burl Jefferson, an enslaved man and resident of Calloway County. Dorris Keeven Franke, a local author and historian, believes there may be an unmarked section of the grave sites of enslaved people in the cemetery.

Thomas Howell Cemetery, Weldon Spring, Missouri

Howell was a leader of area pro-Southerners who was arrested by Arnold Krekel's abolitionist Home Guard. By 1853, Howell enslaved twenty-three people, including Matilda. They all lived in two dwellings, one brick and one log structure. They were buried outside the boundaries of the Howell family plot, and Matilda's grave was probably marked with a plain, rough stone.

There were about 30 people who enslaved at least 10 people in St. Charles County, including David Pitman, William Coshow, Peter Fulkerson, Samuel Keithley and John Talley. In Femme Osage, Calloway and Dardenne Townships, more then 165 families enslaved people.

SAGE CHAPEL CEMETERY, ST. CHARLES COUNTY, MISSOURI (1881)

Mahala (Keithly) and Jasper Castlio transferred one acre of land to the trustees of the African American Episcopal Church so the formerly enslaved people of Samuel Keithley could continue to be buried there. The same deed conveyed one half acre on Sonderen Street for the site of Sage Chapel. The cemetery was also used by members of the nearby African

Sage Chapel Cemetery. *Photograph by the author.*

American Wishwell Baptist and Cravens Methodist Churches. It contains 117 documented burial sites, of which 37 have headstones, along with the burial sites of seventeen people who were born into slavery.

Frances Rafferty Dryden was born into slavery in 1860 and spent a large portion of her life in O'Fallon, Missouri. She was buried in an unmarked grave in Sage Chapel Cemetery. Maria Brady was born into slavery in Missouri and grew up in St. Charles County. She was also buried in Sage Chapel Cemetery. According to local author and historian Dorris Keeven Franke, there are six tombstones marking the graves of formerly enslaved people, at least four of whom were enslaved by Samuel Keithley. Pricella Ball, a formerly enslaved woman, was buried here.

PITMAN CEMETERY, ST. CHARLES COUNTY, MISSOURI

According to Dorris Keeven Franke, there is an unmarked slave burial area in one corner. Archer Alexander was enslaved by the Pitman family.

Pitman Cemetery. Note the yucca plants in the background. *Photograph by the author.*

SECOND GRIFFITH'S GRAVEYARD, ST. CHARLES COUNTY (CIRCA 1839)

This burial ground sits on property that was purchased by Asa Griffith in 1837. It contains the unmarked graves of Daniel Griffith's enslaved people. Daniel, who enslaved quite a few people, had a brick house built on the property in 1836.

CASPER MOLITOR CEMETERY, DOG PRAIRIE (ST. PAUL), ST. CHARLES COUNTY, MISSOURI

This small cemetery contains the burial sites of many of the area's early settlers. Molitor purchased land and built a log cabin near Audrain's Mill. He built an altar inside it, where traveling Jesuit priests from St. Louis would preside on Sundays. Molitor gave a portion of his land for this cemetery. The Hayden family was buried here, and it is thought their slaves were buried here as well.

PRAIRIE HILL PLANTATION, ST. CHARLES COUNTY, MISSOURI

This plantation was purchased by Seth Millington in 1819. The nearby Millington Family Cemetery may contain the unmarked burial sites of their enslaved people.

DAVID BRYAN FAMILY BURYING GROUND, ST. CHARLES COUNTY, MISSOURI

This area contains burial sites of enslaved people. Some people think Nathan and Daniel Boone were buried here, too.

CANNON FAMILY CEMETERY, INDIAN CREEK PARK, ST. CHARLES COUNTY, MISSOURI

The Cannon family settled in this area in 1811. At least nine family members were buried in this cemetery. The earliest burial dates to 1843 (Joseph Cannon). The graves marked by simple fieldstones are possibly those of enslaved people.

FRANCIS HOWELL CEMETERY, ST. CHARLES COUNTY, MISSOURI

Francis Howell Sr. built Howell's Fort by the cemetery in 1800, and a spring was located nearby. He also built a gristmill, which he used to make gunpowder during the War of 1812. His home (demolished in 1941) was close to the fort, with the slave dwellings nearby. Upon his death, one of his enslaved women, Lucy, was freed, according to his will, and provided for from his estate. He bequeathed an enslaved girl, Pleasant, to his son, Francis Jr. Fortunatus Boone Castlio also enslaved several people. It is probable that enslaved people were buried, unmarked, in the cemetery.

DYER/MCMONNIES FAMILY CEMETERY, AREA OF O'FALLON, MISSOURI

This cemetery contains an area with the unmarked burial sites of enslaved people.

OLD FAMILY CEMETERY, HARVESTER, MISSOURI

This cemetery is located behind a house. Nearby are the burial sites of enslaved people marked with plain fieldstones.

Grant Chapel AME Church (1887) and Cemetery (1868), Wentzville, Missouri

The church and cemetery were founded in 1868. The current church building was constructed in 1887. They are located in "Colored Town," or "Need More," which was settled after the Civil War by free Black people. The cemetery contains the burial sites of people who were born before the Civil War—some probably enslaved.

Tunnel Station Cemetery also Known as Fulton-McGuire Cemetery, near Valles Mines, Missouri

McGuire was born in 1773. This cemetery contains the burial sites of formerly enslaved people and area residents.

Parish/Memorial Cemetery, Ste. Genevieve, Missouri (1787)

This extremely old cemetery was given to the Catholics of Ste. Genevieve as a land grant from the King of Spain in 1787. The middle third is the oldest section, which contains burials of Catholics. The third that is located uphill from the middle section is nondenominational and contains the grave sites of Natives and enslaved Black people. Some enslaved Black people are also buried in their enslavers' plots. The cemetery was closed to further burials in 1881.

The cemetery contains the grave of Baptiste, a five-year-old enslaved boy who died in 1787. He was enslaved by Baptiste Valle and buried with the appropriate ceremonies. The burial record was witnessed by the parish priest Louis Guignes. In 1797, the eight-year-old daughter of a chief of the Peoria was buried here. Grave no. 128 on the current guide map is that of "Felix Theodore (slave)" (1825–1847). Cristine, one of the nine people enslaved by Jean-Baptiste LaSource, was buried here. She died in 1783 at around the age of 102. She was never freed. Terese was enslaved by Pierre Aubuchon and was also buried in the cemetery.

Old Salem Church (Salem Methodist Episcopal Church) Cemetery, Ste. Genevieve County, Missouri

The first church burned down, probably in the 1860s. The enslaved were buried in unmarked graves at one end. The earliest death date I could find was 1853.

Buster Cemetery, Valles Mines, Missouri

This is an absolutely fascinating cemetery, with many of its graves belonging to Black people. It contains sunken graves, unmarked fieldstones (possibly the burial sites of the enslaved) and French-style iron cross markers. There is a grave with yucca plants, traditionally found in Black cemeteries. Several markers have inscriptions that look like they were made free hand with a hammer and chisel. One burial is marked with a large cross embedded with cowrie shells on one side, a symbol of prosperity commonly found at Black burial sites. This cemetery is a microcosm of the different ways Black Americans have memorialized their loved ones over the years.

Bisch-Townsend Cemetery ("Colored Creole Cemetery"), Valles Mines, Missouri

This is an old Black cemetery. Sophie McGuire was an enslaved woman in Farmington, Missouri. Her mistress freed her in the middle of the night, and she went to Valles Mines, where she was welcomed and paid for her labor. She was buried behind the General Store/Valles Mines Museum. Her son, John, was also buried there. The Black section of Valles Mines was located at the junction of Highways V and 67. It comprised a church, school and saloon. The area was leveled for the construction of Highway 67.

KENTON'S CEMETERY, VALLES MINES, MISSOURI

Enslaved people were buried in this cemetery. They would have originally had wooden or rough rock grave markers.

OLD JOACHIM CATHOLIC CHURCH CEMETERY, OLD MINES, MISSOURI

This is one of my favorite cemeteries; it's eerie, peaceful, looming and calming all at the same time. It contains tons of old French-style iron cross markers, a couple of New Orleans–style aboveground vaults and sunken graves. There are several markers with small stones embedded in a larger stone form. There are two unusual Art Deco–style grave markers. The T.C. Murphy Mausoleum has a plaque commemorating Henry Murphy, who died in the explosion of the steamboat *Princess* in 1859. Revolutionary War soldiers, including Thomas Madden, were also buried here. The cemetery contains the burial sites of Black people, including those left unmarked for the enslaved. St. Louis and Ste. Genevieve businessmen employed both paid and enslaved labor to work in the mines in the area.

ST. ANN'S CATHOLIC CHURCH CEMETERY, FRENCH VILLAGE, MISSOURI (1828)

George Washington Brooks and his wife, Martha, both formerly enslaved by Salim Grandjean, were buried here. The cemetery has many French-style iron cross markers. The Aubuchons, a very prominent family in the region, were buried here. On the earliest markers, their name is spelled Au Buchon (with a space).

KIMMSWICK CEMETERY, KIMMSWICK, MISSOURI

The lower part of this cemetery, the section closest to the highway, contains the burial sites of enslaved people that were originally surrounded by shells. They are now unmarked.

ST. MARY OF THE BARRENS CHURCH, PERRYVILLE, MISSOURI (1820S)

The original seminary building was constructed in the 1820s, and the church was built in 1827. The seminarians were enslavers. The enslaved were freed over time until around 1860, when one or none were enslaved. To the left of the church is a cemetery and the site of the log cabin church. The graves have since been destroyed or relocated. Now, a lone monument marks the site. According to Jen Kirn, a guide at the church, the cemetery may contain the unmarked grave sites of enslaved people.

APPLE CREEK PRESBYTERIAN CHURCH CEMETERY, PERRY COUNTY, MISSOURI (1822)

This cemetery contains a section of the unmarked burial sites of enslaved people. Some of them were buried in their enslavers' plots. There is a burial record for "Peter McLain, beloved slave of Alexander McLain," in row 28, EE. Alexander's grave is a loose stone vault. He was a Revolutionary War soldier. Many Civil War and Revolutionary War soldiers, along with victims of the 1833 cholera epidemic (unmarked) were also buried here.

James Wilkinson, a Presbyterian from Pennsylvania, was the largest enslaver in Perry County. His home was demolished in the 1940s. One of the locals told me the Catholic church was the second-largest enslaver in Perry County. Enslaved people worked the corn and soybean fields in the area.

MACK'S CHAPEL/SEVENTY-SIX COLORED CEMETERY, NEAR ALTENBURG, MISSOURI

In 1868, William Burford (also spelled "Bufford" or "Buford") was deeded forty acres by his former enslaver. They were initially used as the Burford family's burying ground, which eventually became a cemetery for formerly enslaved farmers who had formed a community in the area called the Mack's Chapel Settlement, or Seventy-Six. A Free Will Baptist church, Mack's Chapel, was associated with the cemetery. The cemetery's last known public service was held in the late 1940s.

JOHNSON FAMILY & SLAVE CEMETERY, CALVEY, FRANKLIN COUNTY, MISSOURI (CIRCA 1840)

Several generations of the Johnson family have been buried in a plot in the center of the cemetery, and enslaved people and free Black people are buried around it. Many fragmented fieldstones are scattered around the central plot. The enslaved labored on a large farm comprising over two thousand acres. The Johnsons' house was located near the cemetery and burned down in 1884. Oral tradition says that the Johnsons purchased and emancipated an enslaved man who had run away from different enslavers and been beaten. The Johnsons granted him permission to be buried in the family's cemetery. Unfortunately, the cemetery has been vandalized in recent years.

BRUSH CREEK CHURCH, NEAR MONROE CITY, MISSOURI

The current limestone church was built in 1862 on the site of an older church, where Augustine Tolton, an enslaved person, was baptized in 1854. Tolton fled Missouri in 1864, after his father joined the Union army. Tolton went on to become the first Black priest in the United States. According to the *Ulysses S. Grant Trail, Missouri, Northeast Segment Official Trail Guide* brochure, the church's graveyard contains the grave sites of enslaved people.

WHITEWATER PRESBYTERIAN CHURCH CEMETERY, SEDGWICKVILLE, MISSOURI (CIRCA 1842)

This congregation was established in 1832. A log church was built in 1842, and acreage for a cemetery was allotted. Enslaved people were buried in unmarked graves in the back part of the cemetery.

HOPEWELL CHURCH CEMETERY, NEAR SEDGWICKVILLE, MISSOURI

The church has since been demolished, but the cemetery is still there. It contains the grave sites of enslaved people. Bollinger Cemetery and Slave House is located nearby. Enslaved people made the bricks for the construction of the house, of which only ruins remain.

BRAZEAU PRESBYTERIAN CHURCH (1852) AND CEMETERY (1832), BRAZEAU, MISSOURI

The first log church burned down in the 1820s, and a new frame church was built by 1833, which was replaced by the current building in 1852. It sports eighteen-inch-thick walls, exposed interior stabilizing rods anchored by tie rods to support the walls and poplar pews from 1853. Unpeeled logs hide under the present-day floor. The bell tower and bells were installed in the 1890s, while the stained-glass windows were placed in 1971. The building still has its original clear etched-glass windows.

This amazing little church contains a rarity—maybe even the only known example of its kind—carvings on the solid wood railings of the slave gallery that were initially made by enslaved people who attended the church and were forced to sit segregated upstairs. The local historian indicated the enslaved people in the area probably had some sort of rudimentary education and were able to write their names and ABCs. Some of the carvings were done in a simple limner style, while others were written in a fancier script, suggesting the earliest carvings were done by the enslaved and, after emancipation, by white or Black children. One carving reads as follows: "1865 Sep." This was the year the Thirteenth Amendment to the United States Constitution was passed, abolishing slavery. There are several names carved in the railings, including "Ida P." Perhaps this name could be found in pre–Civil War slave inventories. Another carved name is "MJ Wilkins." I checked the cemetery records, and there is a white man, Munson Wilkinson, buried in the cemetery. Maybe he never had time to finish carving his last name. Someone practiced the alphabet: "A, B, C, D, E, F, G." Beautiful punched tin walls adorned with trefoil designs representing the Holy Trinity provide a wonderful backdrop for the carvings.

The most fantastic carving is one that I first thought was a diagram of some sort. I took my friends Toi Hatcher and Hattie Felton from the Missouri History Museum there, and Hattie pointed out that it could be a side or front view of the church itself or a barn. It does show a square below the floor, but the church has no basement, just a crawl space. Although I cannot prove it, perhaps this was a hidden room under the church. It is important to remember that Brazeau was mostly pro-Southern, an anomaly in the larger Perry County area. The church was close to the Underground Railroad network around the Liberty Island/Rockwood/Ebenezer Hollow area of Illinois.

The first two burials in the cemetery were held in 1832. The cemetery contains the burial sites of enslaved people, mostly unmarked, and Civil War soldiers. Many enslavers in the area came from North Carolina. James Wilkinson was the largest enslaver in Perry County.

BARBER FAMILY AND SLAVE CEMETERY, NEAR BRAZEAU, MISSOURI

A pair of Barber families arrived in the area ten years apart. The first Barbers enslaved many people. The Barber Family and Slave Cemetery contains the burial sites of enslaved people, which are marked with uninscribed, rough stones. The Barber house was demolished.

NEW LEBANON CUMBERLAND PRESBYTERIAN CHURCH (1859) AND CEMETERY, NEW LEBANON, MISSOURI

In 1812, four preachers, including Reverend Finis Ewing, established the Cumberland Presbyterian Church in Tennessee. Ewing's Kentucky congregation relocated to Cooper County in 1819, calling themselves the "New Lebanon Society." The present meetinghouse was constructed in 1859, with its bricks fired nearby.

The cemetery contains the grave sites of enslaved people, Southern Civil War–era guerillas, Civil War soldiers and two Revolutionary War soldiers.

Pleasant Green Church (1868) and Cemetery, Pleasant Green, Missouri

Local enslaved people, along with their fellow white church members, worshipped in this old church and were buried in its cemetery, which also contains the graves of Union and Confederate soldiers.

In the 1820s, Methodists met for worship in their homes. They built a log church in 1825 near a spring behind Pleasant Green, the house of Winston and Polly Walker, who donated one and a half acres for the church. The cemetery grew up around the church, and in 1836, a larger log meeting house was constructed. In 1868, the current church building was dedicated on one and one-seventh acres provided by Addison and Margaret Walker.

Florence Chesnutt, in *Cooper County Church Sketches* and *The Old Pleasant Green Underground*, wrote that the cemetery contains "box tombs," an English custom brought to Cooper County from Virginia and Kentucky. The Bedwell family of Boonville produced some of the markers, carved with "Heaven's gates," birds and flowers, along with hearses and a team of black horses.

According to Chesnutt, there were several documented burials of enslaved people and their descendants in the cemetery. She notes, "many Negro slaves" were buried there. "Aunt" Dicey (no dates) was enslaved by Dr. J.C. Ewing, while Callie Martin Smith was enslaved by the Walker family. Georgia L. Wilson (1895–1947), who cared for Mrs. Tavenner, was a descendant of people enslaved by the Tavenner family. Plato Young was enslaved by the Walker family and is mentioned in Mary Smith Walker's will. "Young," a daughter of Plato, was also buried there.

Mt. Moriah African Methodist Episcopal Church and Cemetery, Mt. Moriah, Missouri

Florence Chesnutt, in *Copper County Church Sketches* and *The Old Pleasant Green Underground*, noted that the Black members of Pleasant Green Church had started their own African Methodist Episcopal church, Mt. Moriah, by 1850, with a meetinghouse, parsonage and cemetery. Mt. Moriah Road passed through the property of Henry and Winston Walker. Black people had small farms in this area. One of the oldest gravestones in the cemetery shows a birth date of 1832.

During the construction of the Katy Railroad after the Civil War, Mt. Moriah was a Black community complete with a school, cemetery, church and businesses. The residents were self-employed or worked for Swinney Quarry, the railroad or white farmers as sharecroppers.

SUNSET HILLS CEMETERY, BOONVILLE, MISSOURI (CIRCA 1841)

This cemetery began as a Methodist burial ground until it was acquired by Boonville to serve as the city's graveyard. Although the cemetery was not officially established until 1841, burials have taken place here since 1818. It became the de facto place for Black burials after wealthy white people moved their ancestors' graves to Walnut Grove Cemetery. Black Union Civil War veterans are buried here, possibly near a mass grave for white Union soldiers.

"CORN" TAYLOR GRAVE SITE, NEAR PILOT GROVE, MISSOURI

The Cooper County Historical Society's website tells the saga of "Corn" Taylor, who moved, along with his enslaved people, to Cooper County in 1817. He asked to be buried in a local cemetery with his enslaved people, but his request was denied, so he chose to be buried on his own property with over sixteen of his enslaved people. The grave site contains a large marker for Taylor. Researchers counted twenty-nine graves marked only with rough stones.

MT. NEBO BAPTIST CHURCH (1856) AND CEMETERY, PILOT GROVE, MISSOURI

This church was organized in 1820, when around sixty-three people met in a log schoolhouse one mile north of Bunceton. That year, they built a log church and joined the Mount Pleasant Baptist Association. A wood frame church was constructed west of Petite Saline Creek in 1835. In 1856, a new wood frame meeting house was built with a slave gallery in the back (it was removed in 1885). Black congregants enjoyed full membership, regardless of whether their enslavers were church members. Civil War and War of 1812 veterans and enslaved people were buried here.

Wesley Chapel Methodist Church & Cemetery, Pilot Grove, Missouri

In 1883, Frank Johnston, William Hawkins and Anderson Miller bought less than one acre of land next to Mt. Nebo Baptist Church Cemetery for use as a burial ground for formerly enslaved people.

Parks-Foster Cemetery, Camden County, Missouri

This cemetery is located on the Franklin farm. Over one hundred graves have been documented here, including two rows of graves that belong to the enslaved people of the Foster, Davis and Dodson families.

Mace Graveyard, Camden County, Missouri (1820)

Mace family members and their enslaved people were buried here. The graves of the enslaved were marked with uninscribed sandstone rocks. In 1930, the remains of family members were moved to Zion Cemetery in Linn Creek, but the remains of the enslaved were left behind.

Cayce Family Cemetery, Farmington, Missouri

This cemetery has nineteen identified markers. The oldest is that of Pleasant Cayce, who died in 1811. Enslaved people were also buried here.

GEORGE JEWELL CEMETERY STATE HISTORIC SITE, COLUMBIA, MISSOURI (1841)

The two rows of unmarked graves in the back of the cemetery are probably those of the people enslaved by the Jewell family. The cemetery was officially founded in 1841, but there were at least three burials there before that time. The stone wall surrounding the cemetery was built between 1841 and 1852.

WOODLAND/OLD CITY CEMETERY, JEFFERSON CITY, MISSOURI (1837)

Violet and Elijah Ramsey were buried here. Violet was born into slavery in Kentucky in 1796. She was freed by her enslaver in Jefferson City in 1838 and worked as a washerwoman to earn money to buy her husband's and son's (Elijah Sr. and Elijah Jr.) freedom, which she eventually did in 1845. She was able to free another son, Harrison, in 1855.

SAND HILL CEMETERY, NEW MADRID, MISSOURI

Civil War soldiers were buried here in unmarked graves. There is a military tombstone for Civil War soldier Private Orange Spright, Company 1, Fifty-Fifth Regiment, United States Colored Infantry.

DRESDEN BLACK CEMETERY/NORTH DRESDEN CEMETERY, DRESDEN, MISSOURI

This cemetery is located next to the old wooden church building and was probably established in the early 1860s. Formerly enslaved people were buried in this cemetery. The earliest birth date that I could find on a marker is 1838, and the earliest death date is 1905.

FOREST GROVE CEMETERY, LEXINGTON, MISSOURI

Several generations of Black enslaved people and their descendants were buried here.

OLD BAPTIST CEMETERY, HANNIBAL, MISSOURI (1837)

Dea Hoover, in *Hannibal: A Walk Through History*, notes that in 1855, Agness Flautleroy was buried with a lovely headstone that was paid for by her enslaver, Sophia Hawkins, the mother of Mark Twain's good friend Laura Hawkins. Next to Agness's headstone is a marker with "Petunia" roughly carved on it. Hawkins enslaved one person, and the marker may have been placed by her for that person. Both enslaved and free Black people were buried in the cemetery.

PARK VIEW CEMETERY/IRONTON COLORED CEMETERY, IRONTON, MISSOURI (PRE-1860)

Two hundred Union soldiers who mainly perished from disease were buried here, along with at least one Confederate soldier who died at the Battle of Pilot Knob. The remains of these soldiers were moved to Jefferson Barracks National Cemetery in St. Louis in 1867–68. Park View Cemetery later became the main burial site for the area's Black population. Solomon and Moses Lax escaped slavery in 1862. Moses helped build Fort Davidson, and Solomon helped defend it during the Battle of Pilot Knob/Battle of Fort Davidson. The Lax brothers were buried in this cemetery, although Solomon's grave is unmarked.

ST. JOSEPH CITY CEMETERY (SUNBRIDGE CEMETERY), ST. JOSEPH, MISSOURI (1843)

This cemetery started as the city's pauper graveyard. Lloyd Warner, a 1933 lynching victim, was buried in the segregated section. The exact location of his grave is unknown. The paupers' and Black people's graves are also unmarked.

BURIAL SITES OF ENSLAVED PEOPLE IN MISSOURI

FIRST CALVARY CATHOLIC CEMETERY, ST. JOSEPH, MISSOURI

Jeffrey Deroine, a man enslaved by Joseph Robidoux II, was buried here. When the cemetery moved and became Mt. Olivet Cemetery, his grave was lost. Deroine, who was freed by an unknown person for $600 in 1832, was an interpreter for Robidoux in his dealings with the Natives. Deroine played an important role in negotiating the Platte Purchase. Robidoux moved to the St. Joseph area in the 1820s with some of his enslaved people, including Deroine and Poulitte, a cook and manservant.

MT. MORA CEMETERY, ST. JOSEPH, MISSOURI

America Elizabeth Brown (1844–1931), an enslaved girl from St. Joseph, was buried in the northwest section of the cemetery.

SAPPINGTON AFRICAN AMERICAN CEMETERY, ARROW ROCK, MISSOURI

Dr. John Sappington set aside land for the burial of his enslaved people in 1856. Sappington and his extended family enslaved a large number of people. The cemetery contains over three hundred graves, with only seventy-six of them marked. Both enslaved and free Black people were buried here. Around 1834, Dr. Sappington utilized the labor of his enslaved people to manufacture antifever pills (quinine, gum myrrh, licorice) for the treatment of malaria. He made a fortune from the pills. There is a separate Sappington Cemetery nearby for the white family members.

SMITH FAMILY CEMETERY, NEAR LAURIE, MISSOURI

Daniel and Nancy Smith enslaved twelve people. A family they enslaved was buried in the cemetery. One of this family's members, Abner Lacy, left his enslaver late in the Civil War and joined the United States Colored

157

Troops. He was recruited at Tipton. On an overgrown portion of the Leonard's farm, there are ruins of the Freewill Baptist Church and the remains of two cemeteries with grave sites that belong to both Black and white people.

Ray House, Wilson's Creek National Battlefield, Republic, Missouri

A woman who was enslaved by the Ray family was buried on the property. It is the only documented enslaved burial in the Springfield area.

PART III

DWELLINGS OF ENSLAVED PEOPLE IN MISSOURI

God will take care of the poor trampled slave,
but where will the slaveholder be when eternity begins?

—*Sojourner Truth*

7

OVERVIEW

Slavery in the St. Louis area dates to the early eighteenth century, when some of the French and Spanish in the area held Black and Native people in slavery, primarily to work the local lead mines. Nini Harris, a St. Louis historian and author, brought to my attention a series of records at the Missouri Historical Society, some of which pertain to St. Louis. They were translated from French and Spanish in the 1840s so people could establish ownership of property. In the 1930s, a Works Project Administration (WPA) project was established to transcribe the records. The originals disappeared at this time. According to these records, there were both Native and Black enslaved people in St. Louis in 1767. They indicate a man freed one of his enslaved people of mixed ancestry. In 1774, the records show the sale of an enslaved person who was part Black and part Native, healthy and forty-five years old. A few years later, an enslaved person was sold in exchange for animal pelts. Biracial people are listed in these records, including Juanetta and Esther. Around 1800, a Catholic priest bought a Black woman. His intentions are unknown—did he keep her enslaved, or did he free her?

Missouri had "plantations," but for the most part, they were not on the same scale as those in the South. Many were farms that utilized the labor of enslaved people. In some instances, the enslaved lived in segregated spaces within the main house. In other cases, they lived in small, simple outbuildings or in detached kitchen attics. Most of the farms owned by enslavers were situated along the Missouri River from the outskirts of St. Louis and west toward Kansas City. This area was known as "Little Dixie."

There were also some in the bootheel region (southeastern Missouri) and in St. Louis County and City. Hemp was a major Missouri crop before the Civil War, and the enslaved harvested it. The areas surrounding St. Louis were dotted with plantations and farms utilizing enslaved labor, Wildwood and Florissant being examples. St. Charles County also had plantations, including one owned by the Sonderen family. Most Missouri enslavers held fewer than ten enslaved people.

The early settlers in the northern St. Louis area, including along the riverfront, were primarily English and French. Some of them were enslavers. Joseph Brazeau owned land along the Mississippi River, just south of North St. Louis. His enslaved people farmed and operated a lime kiln on the property. The Christys enslaved the largest number of people in northern St. Louis. According to the 1840 census, they enslaved fourteen people. The census lists seventeen additional residents as enslavers.

Several free Black people in northern St. Louis were property owners, like Esther Clamorgan and James Farrar. James Farrar was listed in the 1840 census as a "free male of color" who worked as a gardener and laborer. He died in 1872 at a house on Eleventh and Wright Streets.

In 1860 in St. Louis County, there were around 300 enslaved people in Meramec Township and 412 in Bonhomme Township. Enslavers and Union sympathizers lived close to each other throughout St. Louis County. For example, the Pleasants, who were enslavers, lived in Wild Horse Creek Valley after emigrating from Virginia. Their neighbors included abolitionist Germans who served in the Missouri Home Guard, like Henry and Dietrich Hencken.

In St. Ferdinand Township (Florissant), the enslavers who had at least twelve enslaved people included Reuben Musick (twelve in one dwelling), Franklin Utz (fifteen in two dwellings), Walter B. Morris (eighteen in two dwellings), Frank Rayburn (seventeen in two dwellings), Ann C. Farrar (eighteen in three dwellings), Thomas January (fourteen in two dwellings), Ann B. Jennings (fifteen in one dwelling), Graham (thirty-nine in five dwellings), Jesuit College (twenty-eight in three dwellings) and W.W. Evans (twelve in two dwellings). The enslaved people were crammed into small dwellings, between six and fifteen in each. Graham had five "fugitives," twenty-four Black and fifteen biracial enslaved people, while Frederick Price had a "fugitive" from the state. (The information in this paragraph was taken from *St. Ferdinand Township Census, Enslaved Inhabitants by Slaveholder Household*, June 1860.)

Records of local provost marshals, akin to military police, indicate that an underground network of pro-Southerners was operating in the area now known as Wildwood. In 1862, several locals were arrested near Howell's Ferry for recruiting men for the Confederate army. A military commission decided there was not enough evidence to charge them.

The Fairfax house in Rock Hill (still standing in St. Louis County) was built by James Marshall's enslaved people in 1839. Marshall freed John Purnell and gave him land at the corner of Litzsinger and Lay Roads. Purnell's son lived in the log cabin, which has since been demolished. Marshall also gave land to an enslaved man named Caleb "Cape" Townsend in Webster Groves (St. Louis County). The Bacon log cabin was built by William Bacon in 1835 on a seven-hundred-acre farm that was worked by enslaved people.

The elite of enslavers in St. Charles County included Residing Judge Daniel Griffith (near Cave Springs), Representative Dr. John Talley (near Wentzville) and Senator Edward Bates (on Dardenne Prairie). Enslavers with large "plantation" homes included Bossman Clifton and William McElhiney (most of his enslaved people ran off during the Civil War to enlist in the Union army). In 1840, the largest enslavers in St. Charles County were Taliafero Grantham (thirty-six enslaved), William Preston (thirty-one enslaved) and David Pitman (twenty-one enslaved). Nearby Portage des Sioux had a larger percentage of slaves than St. Charles. Its largest enslaver was Dr. B.F. Wilson (forty-five enslaved).

Eli Keen Sr., a slave catcher, fathered several of his enslaved while living in Kentucky. After his wife, Sarah, died in 1845, he moved to St. Charles County with his sons and enslaved people. Upon his death in 1850, four of his enslaved were freed, including two who were his daughters and a third who was their mother.

According to St. Charles Borromeo Church records, toward the end of Spanish rule, there were a number of free Black people in St. Charles, including Pierre Rodin, who arrived in 1797, probably from the West Indies, and bought three lots and land in the common field.

I owe a debt of gratitude to the research done by Gary Funfhausen on enslaved people's dwellings in the "Little Dixie" region of Missouri. Quarters of the enslaved are extant at the Griot Museum in St. Louis City and in St. Louis County, St. Charles and other areas of Missouri.

8

SITES

FRENCH COLONIAL ERA ST. LOUIS

It is thought by researchers that cabins and barns in the common fields of St. Louis may have served as dwellings for the area's enslaved people in the late eighteenth century. They would have labored in the common areas. A typical layout of the property of a French colonial resident of St. Louis (and Ste. Genevieve) was for the house to be enclosed by a sturdy fence, with outbuildings, including slave dwellings and gardens, inside the enclosure.

In 1779, 150 Ste. Genevieve men enrolled in the Spanish militia. During peacetime, they guarded against Native raids on saltworks and mines and pursued criminals and escaped enslaved people in the region. St. Louis was surrounded to the north, west and south by a trench/palisade (the common fields were outside of it). A circular tower called Fort San Carlos stood where Busch Stadium now stands. In 1780, the British and their Native allies decided to attack St. Louis and Cahokia in order to open the Mississippi Valley to the British. The Spanish leaders in St. Louis had to quickly organize every male they could find—militia members, civilians, free Black people—to defend the city. Ultimately, the St. Louisans were successful in fending off the British. This Revolutionary War engagement was known as the Battle of Fort San Carlos, or the Battle of St. Louis. According to Spanish officials' reports to Madrid, twenty-two settlers, enslaved workers and militiamen were killed, seven were wounded and twenty-four were captured. Some civilians and enslaved workers were killed outside of the trenches in the common fields. Fernando de Leyba, the third governor of Upper Louisiana, decided that if he left the fortifications to rescue those stranded in the common fields, the city would be lost.

According to Robbie Pratte, the director of museum operations at the Center for French Colonial Life in Ste. Genevieve, the enslaved people who died in the Battle of Fort San Carlos were a person enslaved by A. LaPierre, a person enslaved by Gabriel Cerre, another person enslaved by Gabriel Cerre, a person enslaved by Madame Chouteau, a person enslaved by Bonete, a person enslaved by Louis Chancellier and a person enslaved by Pierre Picot de Belestre. The record does not give the names of the enslaved, only those of their enslavers.

Examples of wealthy French colonial–era enslavers in St. Louis are Benito Vasquez and Jean Gabriel Cerre. Jacques Clamorgan built a stone house in 1785, which was bought by Pierre Chouteau in 1788. The entire block on which the house sat was enclosed by a stone fence. The outbuildings inside the fence included structures that were used as fur warehouses, a barn, stables and slave quarters.

St. Louis's original matriarch, Madame Marie-Therese Bourgeois Chouteau, enslaved approximately eight Native people and three Black people. She freed one, Therese, and gave her money, flour and a cow and calf. A public auction of the property of St. Louis's cofounder Auguste Chouteau after he died in 1829 was held at the Old Courthouse and included his enslaved people, of whom thirty-six were sold (probate records, St. Louis Civil Courts, book D, 19). Twelve of these enslaved people were given to Madame Chouteau.

Frenchtown Area of St. Louis City, Missouri

Most of the enslaved in Frenchtown were domestic servants who lived within their enslaver's home. John Rodabaugh, in *Frenchtown*, noted that larger mansions were typically staffed by four enslaved people. John Priest built his house in 1859 for $19,000. He enslaved sixteen people. Neree Valle, a son-in-law of the Chouteaus, gave an enslaved woman, Marie, to his wife as her personal hair stylist. Marie had apprenticed with the well-known hairdresser Jerome Merlin in New Orleans.

Madame Marie-Therese Bourgeois Chouteau enslaved people at both her city house and on her farm on the Grand Prairie. There were dwellings for them at both locations. Some of her enslaved people were killed during the Battle of Fort San Carlos in 1780.

Area Near the Simon Cousset House, St. Louis City, Missouri

This house was a French colonial post-in-ground structure. Near the house was a "slave cabin measuring 20 x 15 pieds" (Michael J. Meyer, "The French of St. Louis: Archaeological Excavation of the Simon Coussot House," *Le Journal*, no. 22 [Fall 2016.])

Robert Campbell House, St. Louis City (1851)

Portions of the following section were taken from an exhibit at the Campbell house titled The Back of the House: Servants & Slavery at Campbell House.

Eliza Rone was an enslaved nursemaid for the Campbell family. She was part of their household by 1845 and was emancipated by Robert Campbell in 1857. He also emancipated her two sons, Aleck and George. Robert's mother-in-law, Lucy Ann Kyle, a Quaker, may have influenced him. Eliza remained at the house as a paid worker until 1867, when she moved to Kansas City, where her husband founded a Prince Hall Masonic lodge and one of her sons worked for a Black newspaper.

According to Director Andy Hahn, while at the Campbell house, Eliza probably lived in a small room on an upper floor in the front portion of the house (now an office).

Pope-Mullanphy House (Taille de Noyer), Grounds of McLuer North High School, St. Louis County (1790)

John Mullanphy purchased Taille de Noyer in 1805. The grounds contained cabins for the enslaved people (now demolished).

In 1860, according to Andrew Theising in *In the Walnut Grove: A Consideration of the People Enslaved in & Around Florissant, Missouri*, John Mullanphy Chambers, the son of Charles Chambers, enslaved eight people in two dwellings at his home (not Taille de Noyer), and Bartholomew Maziere Chambers, another of Charles's sons, enslaved ten people in a single dwelling at Dunmore.

Wright-Smith Plantation Slave Cabin, Originally Located in Jonesboro, Missouri, Now inside Griot Museum, St. Louis

There were around sixteen cabins for the enslaved people at the Wright-Smith plantation in Jonesboro. This cabin was one of three individual units under one roof. One had a fireplace, one was used as a work shed and one was used for curing meat and tobacco.

The Wright-Smith tobacco plantation was settled by Colonel John Smith, a Revolutionary War soldier from Virginia. In 1837, he led a caravan to Missouri that included more than 250 enslaved people. The plantation also served as a stagecoach depot. The dwellings of the enslaved people were built by them using trees on the plantation's property. The enslaved were buried in the plantation's cemetery, most likely in unmarked graves.

Stuart-Utz-Teson House, Hazelwood, Missouri (Circa 1782, the early 1820s)

The construction of this house was begun around 1782 by Joseph St. Germain, a French-Canadian farmer, as a one-room log cabin. Auguste Chouteau, the cofounder of St. Louis, purchased it in 1804. He probably never lived on the property but used the home to house enslaved people who worked his fields. The property was purchased by Alexander Stuart in 1819. He was an enslaver, a territorial and circuit judge appointed by President Madison and a good friend of Lewis and Clark. Stuart expanded the house in the 1820s. According to flovalleynews.com, "Since the property he owned quadrupled in size, he needed to add more room for the slaves who farmed the land. He added another log cabin, extended the roof with dormer windows, created a new enclosed entrance hallway and put in a Creole porch." It is thought by local historians that some of the enslaved people lived in a dwelling attached to the main house at the fireplace for heat. This portion of the house was removed in 1920. There exists a record with the names of the enslaved people who lived here.

The house was purchased by Julius Utz in 1832. Julius and Franklin Utz were Confederate sympathizers. It was said that the saddles of Confederate guerrillas were kept on the home's front porch. Franklin's son, Major James Morgan Utz, a Confederate soldier, was captured at Ballas and Clayton

Roads in St. Louis County on charges of being a Confederate spy. He was found guilty and hanged in 1864. In 2003, the house was moved from its original location at the northwest corner of Utz Lane and Teson Park Drive to Brookes Park.

St. Stanislaus Seminary (1823) and Shrine of St. Ferdinand (Circa 1829–the 1850s), Florissant, St. Louis County, Missouri

St. Stanislaus Seminary was founded by the Jesuits in 1823, when they arrived from their Jesuit plantations in Maryland with six enslaved people: Thomas and Molly/Polly Brown, Moses and Nancy Queen and Isaac and Susan Queen-Hawkins. All six lived in a single-room log cabin. In 1829, two more enslaved families (the Hawkinses and Queens) arrived from Maryland. Anywhere from six to about thirty-five enslaved people resided on the seminary grounds at any one time. Many of them were transferred between St. Stanislaus Seminary, St. Louis College (downtown) and the College Farm north of the city. As punishment, the Jesuits beat and sold away their enslaved people.

In 1833, Thomas Brown petitioned the Jesuits at St. Louis University for his and his wife's freedom. He said he had been "very poorly treated by Rev. Father Verhagen, President of University of St. Louis, who is my present master." His request was denied (shmr.jesuits.org).

The old rock building at St. Stanislaus was built by seminarians and enslaved persons in 1840. According to an antique map of the seminary (Jesuit Archives and Research Center), "cabins for negroes" were located on the seminary grounds (now demolished) near what is now the 700 block of Howdershell Road. There were two cabins for twenty-two enslaved people. The old log cabin was used as a church for free and enslaved Black people.

At the Shrine of St. Ferdinand (circa 1829–the 1850s), the enslaved people of the French and Spanish settlers probably sat in the side and back balconies of the church. These enslaved people built homes in the area by hand.

The Catholics in St. Louis and St. Charles have a long history of enslaving people. For example, Louis DuBourg, the bishop of Louisiana and Florida, purchased an enslaved family in 1822 and later transferred their ownership to Bishop Joseph Rosati. DuBourg gave an enslaved woman, Eliza Nebbit, to Rose Philippine Duchesne, who did great work educating Natives in the region and was canonized in 1988. It must be noted that the area's Catholic sisters did things that were amazingly radical for their time, like educating Black people and participating in Underground Railroad activities (Sisters of St. Joseph of Carondelet).

MICHAEL POWERS FARM, FLORISSANT, ST. LOUIS COUNTY, MISSOURI

In 1859, Powers's property included a home, a smokehouse, a carriage house and slave quarters.

ESTATE OF AIME PERNOD, ST. LOUIS CITY, MISSOURI

Pernod's estate covered sixty-seven acres and included a dwelling for the enslaved, which contained three rooms, each with an outside entrance. It was demolished in 1921. The structure is thought to have been the last standing slave dwelling in the city (not the county).

TWO-STORY BRICK HOUSE ON EDWIN, GLENDALE, ST. LOUIS COUNTY, MISSOURI (MID-NINETEENTH CENTURY)

A detached two-story wooden dwelling for the enslaved people was located on the corner of Elm and Essex Streets. The main house is still there, but the enslaved people's dwelling was demolished.

THOMAS SAPPINGTON HOUSE, ST. LOUIS COUNTY, MISSOURI (1808/1812)

A one-story log cabin on a twenty-by-twenty-foot limestone cellar was built in 1808. A two-story log structure with porches was added around 1812.

A one-story, horizontal log slave cabin was on the 210-acre farm. It was later converted to a chicken house. Recent archaeological excavations have uncovered the footprint of a slave dwelling and detached summer kitchen.

JOHN "JACK" SAPPINGTON FARM, ST. LOUIS COUNTY, MISSOURI (ESTABLISHED IN 1815)

This farm, the largest in the Gravois settlement, sat on the current Westminster Estates, Lindbergh High School and Sappington Acres properties. The main Sappington house was in the area of Coverley Lane in Westminster Estates. A slave dwelling was later moved to Sappington Road.

The largest enslavers in Carondelet Township in the 1850s (enslaving twelve or more people) were Thomas Berry, Joseph Sale, Frederick Dent and John Sappington (U.S. Slave Census for Carondelet Township, 1850s).

ZEPHANIAH SAPPINGTON HOUSE, ST. LOUIS COUNTY, MISSOURI (1805–15)

The property contained a gristmill, tannery, spring house, barn and cabin for enslaved people. The barn was demolished to make way for an apartment complex.

WILLIAM B. HARWOOD HOME, ST. LOUIS COUNTY, MISSOURI (CIRCA 1835)

This log cabin with wood siding was built by William and Martha Harwood on their 225-acre farm. It was the temporary site of services for the newly formed Des Peres Presbyterian Church. There were small cabins for the enslaved people to the west of the house.

Tunstall-Douglass House, St. Louis County, Missouri (Pre-1858)

In 1860, Nicholas B. Douglass enslaved six people. A "slave house" was recorded on the property.

McKnight Farm, Ladue, St. Louis County, Missouri

A brick dwelling for enslaved people was built on the property around 1850. It is the only fully documented slave dwelling in St. Louis County and still stands today.

A slave dwelling at the McKnight farm. *Photograph by the author.*

MARTIN HANLEY HOUSE, CLAYTON, ST. LOUIS COUNTY, MISSOURI (1855)

This house was part of a five-hundred-acre plantation owned by Martin Hanley. According to a lecture given by local historian Sarah Umlauf, Lydia, one of the enslaved women on the farm, was inherited by Cyrene Hanley upon the death of her father, James Walton. The 1855 detached summer kitchen, original to the site, was divided into two sections: one half served as the living quarters for a paid worker and the other half served as the kitchen, where Lydia lived and worked. In 1860, she and her four enslaved children lived there. The property contained additional dwellings for enslaved people that were demolished. Umlauf notes that an 1868 survey map shows the enslaved dwellings.

HAWKEN HOUSE, WEBSTER GROVES, ST. LOUIS COUNTY, MISSOURI (1857)

This house was built by Christopher Hawken, the son of Jacob, who made the famous Hawken rifle, known as "the gun that settled the West." Christopher was an enslaver. His enslaved people included Aunt Molly and Uncle Albert. Some of them may have lived in the sewing room in a back corner of the second floor.

JARVILLE, BALLWIN, ST. LOUIS COUNTY, MISSOURI (1853)

Two early owners of Jarville, the Weidmans and Masons, were enslavers. According to Esley Hamilton, a former St. Louis County historian, aerial views of Jarville and the surrounding area show small outbuildings that may have been slave dwellings.

Frederick Price House, St. Louis County, Missouri (1840s)

This house in north St. Louis County had a rear ell over its kitchen. The upper portion of the ell was used as quarters for the enslaved.

Hazelwood, St. Louis County, Missouri (Circa 1807, Demolished in the 1950s)

The main brick part of this home was built around 1807 and later made into a double house. The last addition was constructed in 1850. It sat on a one-thousand-acre plantation and was used as a hospital during the cholera epidemic of 1833, which took the lives of sixteen of the estate's enslaved people. The dwellings of the enslaved people were located behind the house. Over time, Hazelwood was the home of Reverend William Musick, Major Richard Graham and General Daniel Frost. Graham and his descendants were the largest slaveholders in the township. When Richard Graham died in 1857, he enslaved forty-one people, a large number for Missouri. Malcolm Graham enslaved seventeen people, with thirty-nine more listed under "Graham" (1860 slave schedule).

White Haven (Ulysses S. Grant National Historic Site), St. Louis County, Missouri (1812–16)

Nick Sacco, a park ranger at the Ulysses S. Grant National Historic Site, has done a lot of research on slavery in the region. I am indebted to him for some of the following information. Every owner of this property until 1865 was an enslaver. William Lindsey Long lived there from 1808 to 1818. The people he enslaved built portions of White Haven (the side addition was built in the 1830s by enslaved workers Charles, Jim, Willis and others). When Theodore and Anne Lucas Hunt bought the property from Long in 1818, there were several log cabins there that could be used as slave dwellings. Hunt enslaved five people: Walace, Andrew, Lydia, Loutette and Adie. Frederick Dent, the father of Julia, Ulysses's wife, lived there from 1820 to 1865 and expanded the property to include 850 acres. Per the slave schedules, Dent enslaved thirty people in 1850 (one account indicates he enslaved as many as sixty). Grant enslaved one person, William Jones, who was given to him by Dent. Grant freed Jones in 1859. He also hired out at least two enslaved workers from other farms. Dent gifted four of his enslaved people to Julia: Dan, Eliza, John and Julia (Dent gave his sons tracts of land and his daughters several enslaved people). Julia Grant was accompanied by Jules, an enslaved person, wherever she went, including Galena, Illinois, and Grant's headquarters in Vicksburg. Mary Robinson was an enslaved cook. Old Bob traveled with the Dents from the East Coast to St. Louis and cut wood for the White Haven fireplaces. An 1829 black oak tree still stands on the White Haven property. Perhaps Old Bob worked next to the statuesque old tree. Some of the enslaved men had wives on other local farms, and Frederick Dent gave them permission to visit them.

It is thought by researchers that some of the enslaved people at White Haven lived in the attic of the summer kitchen/laundry. They worked in the winter kitchen, which was located in the basement of the White Haven main house. During archaeological excavations, slate pencils have been found, indicating they may have secretly been learning to write (teaching Black people was outlawed in Missouri in 1847).

Andy Hahn, the director of the Campbell House Museum, found an 1858 record indicating that Grant hired out George, an enslaved man of Francis Sublette. George worked at White Haven in 1858. Around 1864, the enslaved people at White Haven, including Jules, liberated themselves.

According to Emma Dent Casey's memoir, there were eighteen simple log cabins located on the northern part of the White Haven property that served as dwellings for the enslaved there (now the southern portion of Grantwood Village). In 1871, while serving as president of the United States, Grant asked White Haven's caretaker to tear down the slave dwellings.

The enslaved people at White Haven included Jules, who accompanied Julia for most of the Civil War and ran away in 1864, while Julia was away in Kentucky; Old Bob, who accompanied Frederick Dent on the trip from Pittsburgh to settle White Haven; Jim; Charles; Sue; Ann; Hester; Jeff; Willis; Dan; Henrietta Jones; Mary Robinson; and William Jones, the enslaved man of Ulysses. Mary Robinson and Aunt Eadie were most likely cooks, while Kitty and Rose may have been either cooks or nannies. Julia Dent noted that most of the enslaved people came from Virginia and Maryland.

A rudimentary door in the back of the White Haven home, which is still there, was used by the enslaved.

GENERAL DANIEL BISSELL HOUSE (FRANKLINVILLE FARM), ST. LOUIS, MISSOURI (1812–20)

Bissell was the commandant of Fort Bellefontaine and enslaved a large number of people. The house was at least partially built using their labor. There were sixteen cabins for the enslaved people, down the hill to the north of the house, but they were demolished long ago, and modern residences now stand in the location. Nearby, Bellefontaine Methodist Church (1855) contains an extant "slave gallery," which now serves as the choir loft.

Joseph Blake was enslaved by Daniel Bissell in 1815. He had been enslaved in Kentucky before that. He was a brickmaker, plasterer and mason and probably helped build the Bissell house. He ran away in 1816, and Bissell offered a $100 reward for his return in an advertisement he had published in the *Missouri Gazette and Public Advertiser* (April 6, 1816). Per the advertisement, Bissell thought Blake may have gone down the Mississippi River in the direction of Natchez, Mississippi, to find paid work.

CRYSTAL SPRING FARM/WILLIAM RUSSELL HOUSE, ST. LOUIS CITY, MISSOURI (1842)

According to Amanda Clark of the Missouri History Museum, this farm was located at Oak Hill Avenue and Wyoming Street in what is now the Tower Grove South neighborhood. William Russell found coal on his land and established coal mines there. He was an enslaver, and undoubtedly, there would have been dwellings for the enslaved people on the property. Oak Hill was an area of farms, orchards and mines, and other farms in the area had enslaved people and dwellings for them.

Washington Reed is referenced in William Russell's agricultural records from 1835. Reed was there as early as that year. He ran away twelve years later. Russell published an advertisement for the return of Washington; his wife, Mary; and their children, Fielding, Matilda and Malcolm. It indicated they were on their way to Chicago via a covered wagon and were being assisted by a white conductor. Reed was described as thin, upright and well dressed. It was also said that he was carrying an ivory-capped cane.

Thornhill (Governor Frederick Bates House), Faust Park, St. Louis County, Missouri (1817–19)

The Bateses' enslaved people included Ben, worth $350, who worked in the blacksmith shop and earned a good deal of money for Governor Bates. It is speculated that the Bateses' enslaved people lived in the basement of the main house, on the second floor of a detached kitchen or on the site of a current subdivision to the south of the house. The small cemetery behind the house may contain the burial sites of enslaved people, but there is no documentation regarding this.

According to the Thornhill brochure published by the St. Louis County Parks Department, the Bateses purchased Sam and Polly and their son, Juno. Bates wrote a letter to his mother stating that they were successful in farming the property. He promised her not to punish his enslaved people, as she was an antislavery Quaker. An 1818 letter to Frederick from his brother Edward states that while traveling from Virginia to St. Louis, Edward used Ben, Frederick's enslaved blacksmith, as a driver. Ben most likely came from the estate of Thomas Bates, Frederick's father. In 1820, Frederick purchased Lucy and Silva, and in 1824, he purchased Winney and her children, Hannahretta, Mary and Harriet. The 1825 estate inventory of Frederick lists the following enslaved people: Benjamin; his wife, Winnie; and their children, Henrietta, Mary, Harriet, Margaret, Silva and Lucy.

Cayce House, Farmington, Missouri

Jeannie Roberts of Farmington (cited in *History of Slaves* by Roger Forsyth on sites.routweb.com) said there was a tunnel from her house leading under the street to the Cayce house. The Cayces were enslavers, and their enslaved people lived in quarters behind the family house (later rebuilt as a shed).

According to oral tradition, a six-foot-square monument located off Fredericktown Road served as a mass grave marker built by the enslaved people of early Spanish settlers.

The Cedars, Barnhart, Missouri

A two-pen dogtrot log slave dwelling on the property was photographically documented by the Historic American Buildings Survey in the 1930s.

Coleman and Tyler Plantations, Wildwood, Missouri

The District of St. Andre (Meramec Township) had a population of 393 in 1798, most Americans, with 20 percent being enslaved. Wildwood was in Meramec Township, which, in 1850, had a population of two thousand; 51 percent had southern roots, and 23 percent were enslaved. In 1870, 17 percent were Black.

Meramec Township newspapers contained advertisements for freedom seekers before the Civil War. These advertisements were usually marked with the image of a Black-silhouetted traveling Black man or woman. For example, James or John Ball placed an advertisement in a local newspaper around 1836 for a freedom seeker.

In 1837, the Reverend Robert Coleman and Henry Tyler families left Virginia for Missouri with more than one hundred of their enslaved people. Robert's son, William, kept a log of the journey. He indicated that the Colemans and Tylers traveled by horse and carriage, but the enslaved had to walk. The enslaved ranged in age from early childhood to their forties and fifties. The journey took just under two months. After arriving in Wild Horse Creek Basin, Coleman established a 900-acre plantation, and Tyler established a 1,024-acre plantation. The main crop of both was hemp. After Coleman died in around 1842, the property was divided between his two sons, Robert G. and William. By the 1840s, Tyler's plantation included fifty-two enslaved people and over 1,000 acres, with a primary crop of hemp. Henry Tyler's house (circa 1837) is still standing.

Robert G. Coleman was a state senator and leading member of the Missouri secessionist movement. In 1850, he lived in his father's house on a Missouri River bluff west of the Coleman Slave Cemetery. His property was valued at $6,000, while that of Henry Tyler was worth $10,000. Robert enslaved thirty-six people and raised a variety of crops, the main cash crop being hemp. By 1860, he owned a 440-acre plantation, with forty enslaved people living in eight houses. William's mansion, located southwest of the

Coleman Slave Cemetery, was called "Mount Comfort" and dated before 1849. It was demolished in the 1950s.

The Tyler property contained a slave jail. There were chains and rings in the basement of the William Coleman house that were used to punish the enslaved people by forcing them to sit in the dark for a week on a stool while chained to the wall. This information was provided to local historian Bill Kennedy by a Coleman granddaughter. According to a long oral family tradition, William harbored Confederate troops at his plantation.

The Robert Coleman and Henry Tyler families shared a family cemetery southeast of the Coleman plantation.

EATHERTON PLANTATION, WILDWOOD, MISSOURI

The Eatherton family moved with their enslaved people to the Wildwood area from Virginia. Dwellings of the enslaved would have been located on the property. The plantation gatekeeper's house is still there, and its interior retains the original walnut paneling.

FIRST MISSOURI STATE CAPITOL STATE HISTORIC SITE, ST. CHARLES, MISSOURI

This structure served as Missouri's capitol building from 1821 to 1826. The foundations of several outbuildings (two wells/cisterns and two utility buildings) were excavated behind the capitol building. One of the larger outbuildings may have been a summer kitchen, storage shed or dwelling for the enslaved. Workers at the capitol building indicated there is a foundation for a brewery or carriage house on the property. The earliest record of the site is an 1886 Sanborn map.

ABSALOM WHITE'S HOUSE, ST. CHARLES, MISSOURI (CIRCA 1850)

Absalom White was a formerly enslaved man who lived next to the Madison Street Church, a Black church built by enslaved people around 1855 that was renovated into a residence in 1947. After being freed, White was lynched for preaching the Gospel. Workers found his "freedom papers" hidden under the stairs of his home.

About half a block west of the Madison Street Church was the Powell house. Powell was an enslaver. He built a tunnel from his home to the church so his enslaved people could attend church without getting in trouble with the law. There were probably slave dwellings located on the Powell property.

MAGPIE'S, ST. CHARLES, MISSOURI (CIRCA 1812)

Stucco now covers the original brick walls of this old building. An extant detached brick summer kitchen behind the house served as a slave dwelling with a built-in brick oven. The enslaved lived on the second floor and worked on the first floor. According to local author and historian Dorris Keeven Franke, Unionist Arnold Krekel lived in the building directly to the north and across the side street (Charles Tayon had sold the property in 1812). It was also used as a provost marshal's office. A small attachment at the back of the structure was built well before the main house and may have served as a dwelling for Tayon's enslaved people. The title of the property on which Magpie's sits was proofed to Tayon in 1821. He was deeded land in St. Charles County as a reward for his service during the defense of Fort Joseph. He was the civil commandant (Spanish governor) of St. Charles from 1793 to 1801 and fought in the Battle of Fort San Carlos in St. Louis in 1780. The mill building across the street from Magpie's was a hospital and prison during the Civil War.

"COLLIER'S COTTAGE," NEXT TO NEWBILL-MCELHINEY HOUSE, ST. CHARLES, MISSOURI

Catherine Collier was a civic leader, educator and the founder of a Methodist church and St. Charles College. In the early nineteenth century, Collier's Cottage served as living quarters and a school for enslaved people. Collier was not an enslaver and should be commended for educating Black people.

CRIBBENS-KUHLMANN HOUSE, ST. CHARLES COUNTY, MISSOURI (1857)

According to Amy Haake, an archivist for the St. Charles County Historical Society, outbuildings shown on an 1875 plat map were originally slave dwellings.

FORT ZUMWALT, O'FALLON, MISSOURI (1798 AND 1884)

This property was bought by the Healds from Jacob Zumwalt in 1817. The Healds enslaved more than fifty people. A 1912 photograph of the fort shows a small log building behind the fort's eastern portion that was possibly used as a dwelling for enslaved people. During archaeological excavations led by Joe Harle in 2004, light blue azure beads were found. Black people used this color to ward off evil spirits.

DANIEL BOONE HOUSE, DEFIANCE, MISSOURI (1804–10)

This was the home of Nathan Boone, one of Daniel's sons, and the last permanent residence of Daniel Boone. The Boones enslaved people on the property. The lower level of the house contains the dining room and cooking area. A pass-through in the wall was used by the enslaved people when cooking and serving meals.

Daniel, Daniel Morgan and Nathan Boone were all enslavers. Daniel Morgan brought enslaved people to Defiance in 1797 to start work on a small building. They may have later helped build the Daniel Boone house. Daniel Morgan lived nearby and may have lent his enslaved people to Daniel. In 1837, Nathan took his enslaved people with him when he moved to Ash Grove, near Springfield, Missouri.

There were two log cabins on the site before the large main house was built. Nathan's wife, Olive, made her enslaved girl lay the floor in one cabin. Once the main house was completed, the two cabins may have been used as slave dwellings. Nathan enslaved nine people on the property. His brother, Daniel Morgan Boone, who lived nearby, enslaved twenty people.

BOONE FARM, NEAR PHILADELPHIA, MISSOURI

This farm was built by the descendants of Daniel Boone. The basement served as the dwelling area for the enslaved people. There were supposedly chains in the ceiling.

SYLVAN VILLA PLANTATION, "LITTLE DIXIE" AREA, MISSOURI (1830s)

This was one of the Swinney family's plantations (others include Hazel Ridge, circa the 1840s; Villa Plantation, 1860; and the "Big House," 1860). All have been demolished. Sylvan Villa was a tobacco plantation with sixty-nine people enslaved by Captain Swinney. Dwellings of the enslaved would have been located on the grounds of each of these plantations.

HAZEL RIDGE PLANTATION, NEAR GLASGOW, MISSOURI (1840s)

This plantation was owned by the Swinney/Morrison family, and the grounds would have included quarters for the enslaved people.

MAPLEWOOD PLANTATION, BOONE COUNTY, MISSOURI (1830s)

This plantation belonged to the Lenoir family. Dwellings of the enslaved people would have been located on the grounds.

HISTORIC ROBERT M. CRAIGHEAD PLANTATION & CEMETERY, NEAR FULTON, CALLOWAY COUNTY, MISSOURI (1820–21)

Robert Craighead and his wife, Nancy Powell, arrived in Calloway County from Franklin County, Virginia, in 1819. On their journey, they spent the winter in St. Louis to care for an ill child. In the meantime, an older son, accompanied by the family's enslaved people, built log cabins at the farm site, which comprised several hundred acres.

Log slave dwellings (now demolished) sat to the east and west of the Federal-style mansion, which was built using bricks fired on the grounds by the enslaved. Craighead enslaved thirty-six people in 1830, twenty-one in 1841 and twenty-two in 1850.

The mansion is a showcase of early nineteenth-century construction techniques. It sports eighteen-inch-thick walls and a third-floor attic. The second-floor ceiling is composed of hand-made walnut beams. The cellar features overhead walnut logs leveled at the top to support the main floor. One cellar wall is extended to support the fireplace. Part of the original house was demolished, and a front porch was added. The Craigheads planted numerous evergreen trees and kept a garden near the house planted with honeysuckle, pinks and other flowers. In 1821, the first meeting of the Court Street Methodist Church of Fulton was held in the mansion. An early cemetery with interesting markers sits near the house. It is likely the family's enslaved were buried in unmarked graves in the area.

Robert Craighead was recorded as the third taxpayer in Calloway County in 1824 and served on the first grand jury called there.

OLD OAKS PLANTATION (SLUSHER HOUSE), LAFAYETTE COUNTY, MISSOURI

This plantation included the main house, outbuildings and dwellings for the enslaved, which were demolished in 2007.

PRAIRIE PARK PLANTATION, SALINE COUNTY, MISSOURI (1845–49)

Prairie Park was the 2,300-acre hemp and livestock plantation of William B. Sappington, who enslaved about thirty-eight people. The enslaved fired the bricks for the house from clay on the property. The hole where the clay was removed became the basement of the house. There were originally about twenty-four dwellings for the enslaved people on the property. The domestic workers lived in the "nicer" brick structures closer to the main house, while the field laborers resided in rougher buildings farther away from the main house. A shackle still hangs from a basement wall of the main house, and original bars still cover the basement windows.

Three surviving dwellings of the enslaved are shown in a plate from *Treasured Views of Saline County Atlas: Bird's-Eye Views* (1876) that shows the plantation. The three dwellings are a brick building near the main house, a kitchen behind the house (now attached to it with a corridor; originally a detached summer kitchen) and a wooden structure that had later lean-to additions built on either side. This last structure still has patches of "haint blue" (a traditional African color) paint visible inside.

The Prairie Park Plantation house. *Photograph by the author.*

The kitchen, which was originally detached from the main house, where the enslaved worked at Prairie Park Plantation. *Photograph by the author.*

Above: A brick slave dwelling at Prairie Park Plantation. *Photograph by the author.*

Left: The original door and wall with traces of "haint," or blue paint, of a frame slave dwelling at Prairie Park Plantation. *Photograph by the author.*

BURWOOD PLANTATION, NEAR PILOT GROVE, MISSOURI (CIRCA 1830)

The current Queen Ann–style house was built in 1880 on a plantation that was started in around 1830 by Henry Rubey Walker. It was composed of eight hundred acres and backed up to Pleasant Green Plantation. The original brick house and combination slave dwelling and summer kitchen were built round 1830. Henry Rubey Walker II inherited the plantation, which included the brick main house, a combination slave dwelling and summer kitchen and a three-room slave dwelling (circa the 1850s). In 1880, he built a new wood frame house on the foundation of the original house. The combination slave dwelling and detached summer kitchen was incorporated into the back of the new home. The three-room slave dwelling still stands behind the house. Fragments of the original wall covering still hang inside it. In 1860, Henry Sr. enslaved twenty people in five dwellings.

CRESTMEAD PLANTATION (PRAIRIE VIEW), NEAR PILOT GROVE, MISSOURI (1857–59)

This plantation was built in the Italianate style by John Taylor. A recent fire destroyed much of the house, but it was rebuilt. By 1860, Taylor enslaved nineteen people in four dwellings on 4,600 acres. A combination slave dwelling and summer kitchen still stands behind the house.

PLEASANT GREEN PLANTATION, NEAR PILOT GROVE, MISSOURI (1820)

The Walker family arrived in the Pleasant Green Valley area of Cooper County, Missouri, from Kentucky in 1820. They brought two Black families with them. The Walkers settled on a Spanish land grant of hundreds of acres that was given to Winston's father, Samuel Walker Sr. The family collectively owned thousands of acres of land and enslaved over seventy-six people. By 1860, Anthony Walker enslaved thirty-two people in five dwellings on thirteen thousand acres. His enslaved people raised livestock and labored in hemp, tobacco and corn fields. Some of them enlisted in the Union United States Colored Troops during the Civil War, and some ran away.

Winston and Polly Walker's mansion, Pleasant Green, was built around 1820, with Federal-style additions constructed of brick made on the property by the enslaved people (1835 and 1850). A dwelling for the enslaved people still stands behind the main house. In 1877, three dwellings of the enslaved were located on the property (there were five originally). One original dwelling, which has since been demolished, was a detached combination summer kitchen/dwelling constructed of logs. The Walkers held a total of sixty-one enslaved people on several plantations living in ten dwellings.

Additional Dwellings of the Enslaved in the Little Dixie Area

The Elliot house (circa the 1840s) in Boonville had a dwelling attached to the main house. The Anderson house in Lafayette County had a detached two-story wood frame dwelling with six to eight rooms that housed most of the forty enslaved on the property. The Smith farm in Boone County included an enslaved dwelling that housed Ann, among others.

Abbingdon Plantation, South of Foristell, Missouri

According to local author and historian Dorris Keeven Franke, the Abbingdons came from Virginia in the 1830s and brought their enslaved people with them. In the 1850s, Henry Abbingdon fathered a child with Sally, a thirteen-year-old enslaved girl. A cabin that is still standing on the property may have served as the quarters for the enslaved.

Plantation of Missouri Pro-Southern Governor Claiborne Fox Jackson, Howard County, Missouri

Slave censuses indicate Governor Jackson enslaved twenty people in 1850 and forty-eight people in 1860. They lived in eight dwellings.

Russel Reinhard House, Lexington, Missouri

This property contained a two-story detached summer kitchen that also served as quarters for the enslaved people.

Winsor-Aull House, Lexington, Missouri (1851)

This Greek Revival mansion was built by Thomas Winsor, who owned three enslaved people in 1850. Their quarters were built around 1851.

Hicklin-Hearthstone, Lexington, Missouri (Circa 1838)

This one-thousand-acre plantation had two slave dwellings in 1838. Angela da Silva, a St. Louis historian, says it is the "only intact slave-breeding plantation in the country." It had a five-cell birthing cabin and overseer's cabin.

Todd Hunter House, Lexington, Missouri (1839)

The original part of this house was built by John Waddell. It was made of timber frames with walnut clapboard siding. The rear section was added in the 1840s. The original portion contains a living room and parlor on the main floor and two bedrooms upstairs. The dining room and kitchen are located in the 1840s rear section. The space above them served as quarters for the enslaved, accessible only by an enclosed stairway on the back porch.

Eversole House (Village Hall), Caledonia, Missouri (Circa 1855–57)

There is a slave dwelling in this home's backyard.

Ruggles/Evans/Dent House (Now Caledonia Bed and Breakfast), Caledonia, Missouri (Circa 1849)

The former quarters of the enslaved are located above this home's keeping, or receiving, room. At one time, twelve to fourteen enslaved people lived at the house.

Stage Stop Inn, Caledonia, Missouri (1824)

This structure was built by Jacob Fisher. The back of the house had separate quarters for the enslaved people. In the late 1840s, tunnels connected it to the Jane Thompson house (1848) and Ruggles house (1849). The tunnels went under the current Highway 21 to a creek. At one time, enslaved people were owned jointly by families in the three homes, and they used the tunnels to get to the fields to work. During the Civil War, the Stage Stop Inn served as a Union hospital for injured soldiers from the Battle of Pilot Knob. It is now the Wine Cottage Bed and Breakfast and Twelve Mile Creek Emporium.

By 1860, Jane Thompson owned 525 acres and enslaved five people. There was a brick dwelling for the enslaved people behind her house that was photographed by the Historic American Buildings Survey in the first half of the twentieth century.

Morse Mill Hotel, Morse Mill, Missouri (1816)

This home was originally a residence and later a hotel. The limestone wall in front of the house was hand carved by enslaved people. It served as a Confederate field hospital during the Civil War. Quarters for the enslaved people were later used for storage and as a wine cellar.

Kendrick House, Carthage, Missouri (1854)

This home was built using the labor of enslaved people. The property contained brick dwellings for the enslaved. The house had a frame addition on the rear that was used as a dining room, kitchen and quarters for the enslaved people (it was demolished in 1908). There were rumors that enslaved people were murdered on the property, including one woman who was hanged in the backyard. The main house was occupied by soldiers during the Civil War, as two battles were fought in Carthage (1861 and 1864). The Union army burned the porch. Local tradition says there is a trapdoor in the living room floor that leads to a tunnel.

The 1860 Newton County slave census shows that William Kendrick enslaved a thirty-seven-year-old Black woman and six children.

GREEN TREE TAVERN (JANIS-ZIEGLER HOUSE), STE. GENEVIEVE, MISSOURI (1790)

This French Colonial poteau-sur-sole (post-on-sill) home was built by Nicolas Janis, a French-Canadian fur trader who arrived in Kaskaskia from Quebec. He came to St. Genevieve in 1790. At that time, records indicate he enslaved nineteen people. The 1791 census taken by the Spanish government reports he enslaved ten people on the property. His enslaved people would have built the main house and outbuildings. His son, François, inherited the house and converted a portion of it into a tavern in the late 1790s and early nineteenth century. In 1833, the house was purchased by Mathias and Barbara Ziegler. According to the superintendent of the Ste. Genevieve National Historical Park, Chris Collins, the raised basement of the house was used as living quarters for the enslaved people of Nicolas Janis.

Archaeological excavations have been conducted at the location of one of the outbuildings since 2006. It was a poteaux-en-terre structure that most likely had a brick chimney. The windows would have had glass. The study concluded the building was probably used for domestic activities and would have served as a slave dwelling, a detached kitchen or both. The entire Janis property would have had a palisade-like fence around it, enclosing the orchard, barn, hen and goose coops, vegetable garden, stable, detached kitchen and slave cabins.

Tandy Thomas, the director of the board of the Center for French Colonial Life in Ste. Genevieve, told me that a recent archaeological excavation revealed a large baking oven (circa 1780–1820) that may have been communal and possibly used by enslaved people.

Some of the well-known families of Ste. Genevieve County were enslavers, including the Valle, Janis, Beauvais, Chouteau, Amoureux, Rozier, St. Gemme, Menard and Guibord families. There were at least sixteen women enslavers. The people who enslaved the largest number of people were Thomas Bryant (twenty-four enslaved), Antoine Janis (eighteen enslaved) and W.A. Bridgeman (seventeen enslaved). The information in this paragraph is gleaned from the 1860 slave census (Slave Inhabitants in the County of Ste. Genevieve). The records were handwritten, so the names can be difficult to read and some spellings may be incorrect.

The townships covered by this census were Saline, Beauvais, Union and Ste. Genevieve, along with the town of St. Mary and city of Ste. Genevieve.

The 1850 slave census (Slave Inhabitants in the County of Ste. Genevieve) includes the prominent names of Bolduc, Janis, Rozier, Valle, Menard and St. Gemme. It also includes the names of at least eighteen women enslavers. The people who enslaved the largest number of people were J. Coffman (fifty-two enslaved), John Coffman (twenty-five enslaved) and Joseph Griffiths (fifteen enslaved). The townships covered by this census were Ste. Genevieve, Beauvais, Saline, Union and Jackson, along with the city of Ste. Genevieve.

In the 1850s, the St. Mary's Road Enclave, a community of free Black people, was formed in the vicinity of the Amoureux and Ribault houses. The Amoureuxes were prominent members of this community.

FELIX VALLE HOUSE AND JACQUES GUIBORD HOUSE, STE. GENEVIEVE, MISSOURI

Each house on this property has an extant detached slave dwelling. These houses are open to the public for tours, and much information pertaining to them can be found on the internet.

Isaac and Joseph, two of the freedom seekers involved in the 1852 "slave stampede" discussed earlier in this book, likely lived in the dwelling for the enslaved at the Felix Valle house.

The homes of Louis Bolduc, Nicolas and Francois Janis, Vital St. Gemme Beauvais and the Valle brothers were built using the labor of their enslaved people in the late eighteenth century. Jean-Baptist Beauvais enslaved thirty people, whom he brought to Ste. Genevieve from Kaskaskia. Their dwellings (now demolished) were located in the yard of the Beauvais-Amoureux house.

LOUISIANA ACADEMY, STE. GENEVIEVE, MISSOURI (1808)

There were many log dwellings of the enslaved on this property until 1935, when they were demolished for a high school building.

JOSEPH PRATTE WAREHOUSE, STE. GENEVIEVE (CIRCA 1820)

This warehouse comprised two limestone buildings connected by a rounded central archway. It ran along an outer edge of Pratte's property and functioned as a fence/stockade. It also served as quarters for the enslaved people. In the twentieth century, it was called the "Rock School." The building was demolished, and the stones were used by a local artist to build a studio.

VALLES MINES, MISSOURI

George Washington Brooks was born into slavery in 1853. At the age of seven, he was gifted to a family in French Village, Missouri, near Valles Mines. After slavery was abolished, he worked as a servant for a family there for the rest of his life.

DANIEL BOONE HAYS HOUSE, NEAR DEFIANCE, MISSOURI (1836–38)

Hays, Daniel Boone's grandson, enslaved three to four people, one of whom worked in the attached kitchen on the main floor. A staircase in the kitchen led to a second-floor room, which served as the quarters for the enslaved. Only the enslaved used these stairs, the only way to access the second-floor room. The guide said there were originally log cabins on the property, and one or more may have served as quarters for the enslaved people. A display in the home indicates there was a "slave cabin" on the property.

Saxon Lutheran Memorial, Frohna, Missouri

Frohna was founded in 1839 by Lutherans from Saxony, Germany. The property includes a log cabin (the 1820s/1842/1870/1913), a log barn, a pair of small log buildings, a granary, a machine shed, a two-story log cabin and a pair of single-room log cabins. The pair of small log buildings served as slave dwellings in the 1820s, before the arrival of the Germans.

Faherty House, Perryville, Missouri (1827–31/1854)

This home was built on one of the original town lots as a two-room stone house with a basement. Two rooms with brick walls were added in 1854. It was most likely built for Henry Burns Sr., an enslaver born in Kentucky. The enslaved people lived in a small stone cabin behind the house.

Danville Female Academy, Danville, Missouri (Opened 1853)

This school was established by Reverend James Robinson. Only the chapel remains today. The original complex consisted of a school building with recitation rooms, a chapel, three dormitories with parlors and music rooms, and dining halls, all arranged in a semicircle. Cabins for the enslaved people were located nearby. In his article on the 1874 raid on Danville, Corey Orr quotes Mary Lee Kemper, who published reminiscences from her mother's notes: "The cabins for the negro servants [enslaved] were standing some distance off from the other houses." Kemper's mother, Mary Robinson, was a student at the academy.

W.G. Downing Mansion, Memphis, Missouri (1858)

Downing brought twelve enslaved men and women from Virginia to Memphis, Missouri. They built the foundation of Downing's house below the frost line, seven feet deep, with a footing, and made the bricks for the house in a kiln on the property, near the pickle factory. The enslaved dwellings were located behind the main house.

During the Civil War, Downing's home was taken over by the Union army. The soldiers camped on the property. Legend says they rode horses inside the house. Horseshoe marks were visible on the original pine floors (now covered with oak flooring). Oral tradition says that a Union soldier, Dr. Aylward, was hanged on the Downing farm.

Thatcher-Woods Farm, Clay County, Missouri (1833)

A private girls' school and the family cemetery are now located on the property. Slave cabins were located near the main log house (which was demolished in 2015).

Darwin-Adkins House, Clay County, Missouri (1859)

The brick for the main house was made on the property, a 320-acre hemp plantation with six slave dwellings.

Bingham-Waggoner Estate, Independence, Missouri (1852)

Lewis, this estate's original owner, was an enslaver. The dwelling of the enslaved, a two-story wooden building, was situated near the main house. The famous artist George Caleb Bingham used it as his studio from 1864 to 1870. It was demolished in 1902.

House on North Leonard, Liberty, Missouri (1850)

This home once served as a honeymoon cabin, which had an embossed bathroom ceiling. The current garage was once a slave dwelling.

Manheim-Goldman House, Liberty, Missouri (Circa 1859)

The older front portion of this home was built around 1859. The small building west of it was a summer kitchen, which probably served as slave quarters.

Villa Kaitlyn, Liberty, Missouri (1830s, 1860)

Portions of this house, including the wing, date to the 1830s. The property originally contained a lake, an apple orchard and a barn. A small building across the street is one of the property's slave dwellings.

Stephen's House, Boonville, Missouri (1846)

The bricks for this home were made on-site. There was a small cabin located behind the house that was used as a slave dwelling.

Vuille/Grandjean Slave Cabin, Valles Mines, Missouri

This structure currently sits behind the general store in the historic portion of Valles Mines. It was relocated from an area farm owned by Aime Ament Vuille and then his nephew Salim Grandjean, who converted it into a granary around 1870. There were five dwellings for the enslaved on the original farm site, 440 acres located at the far eastern end of Valles Mines. Two of the family's enslaved people, George Washington and Martha Brooks, lived on the second floor of the main brick house. Salim was married to Emily Aubuchon. The Aubuchons were a well-known area family.

Joe Casey was born enslaved in Washington County. He was the last enslaved person at Valles Mines. His pre–Civil War home is still standing in the historic section of town.

Steven Frazier, the historian at Valles Mines, indicated the miners taught the enslaved people to read and write in the mines. They called it the "Underground School of Valles Mines." Frazier provided some of the information about the Valles Mines sites.

Colonel Benjamin Stephenson House, Edwardsville, Illinois (1820)

I came across this home while researching slave dwellings in Missouri. In 1820, Colonel Stephenson enslaved seven people. A guide at the 1820 Colonel Benjamin Stephenson house indicated the enslaved people lived in the attic of the detached kitchen (still extant), where they worked.

J. Huston Tavern, Arrow Rock, Missouri

A detached kitchen with an open-hearth fireplace (circa the 1850s) was later incorporated into the main building. The loft of the kitchen most likely served as the living quarters for the enslaved cook. A similar arrangement is evident at the Miller-Bradford house. Enslaved people made the bricks and sawed the lumber on-site for the construction of the tavern. Joseph Huston and his brother Benjamin did the carpentry work. Freedom seekers passed through Arrow Rock on their way to Kansas, Iowa and Illinois, but there were no official safe houses in the town.

Rice-Tremonti Farm, Raytown, Missouri (1844)

This property contains an 1830s slave cabin. The farm was a campsite for travelers heading west on the Oregon and California Trails.

John Wornall House, Kansas City, Missouri (1858)

In 1860, John Wornall enslaved four people. After 1863, he paid them, probably to keep them from running away. But this did not work, and they fled to Kansas. The Wornall family lived in a small house on the property until the larger house could be finished. The smaller house was most likely used as a dwelling for the enslaved once the Wornall family moved into the larger house.

St. Clair Dimmitt House, Liberty, Missouri (1869, 1871)

The brick building behind the house was built circa 1848–56 and served as a kitchen and living quarters for the enslaved people. It consisted of two back-to-back rooms, each with a fireplace vented by a central chimney. Dimmitt was a merchant and hemp planter.

Iberia Academy, near Lake of the Ozarks, Miller County, Missouri

This property contains an 1830s slave cabin. John and his wife were among the enslaved people who called this cabin home. The academy was remodeled and expanded in 1890. There are many grave sites on the property.

Elmwood Farm and Home (Now Someplace Inn Time), Palmyra, Missouri (1853)

This land was originally owned by Andrew Muldrow, who purchased it in 1848. The house was built by John and Catherine Garner, who lived there until 1867. Enslaved people worked the eighteen-acre property. The outbuildings on the property included a summer kitchen, a granary, a stone barn, a pole barn and a dwelling place for the enslaved people, which had two rooms, plus an attic. A fireplace was located in one room. The back rooms of the main house were accessible only from the outside and housed the domestic enslaved people. The house served as a hospital during the Civil War.

KASKASKIA, ILLINOIS

New Kaskaskia developed in the second half of the nineteenth century three miles south of Old Kaskaskia after the old town suffered many disastrous floods.

In 1675, the Jesuit Parish of the Immaculate Conception was founded by Father Marquette at Starved Rock, Illinois (Utica). He established a mission to convert the Kaskaskia to Catholicism. They moved south along the Mississippi River to Peoria and then to a site on the River Des Peres in St. Louis in 1699. Due to threats of a Native attack, they again moved to Old Kaskaskia with missionary Father Marest in 1703. Their enslaved people, both Native and Black, worked the land of the Jesuit plantation at Kaskaskia and labored in the brewery and flour mills. They were allowed to attend services and get married and baptized at Immaculate Conception Church. The first church building was constructed in 1714. The current building dates to 1843. It was moved to New Kaskaskia in 1894.

In 1720, the Jesuits at Kaskaskia enslaved about seventeen people, both Black and Native. The Kaskaskia Jesuits and seminary priests at Cahokia were the largest enslavers in Illinois Country. They obtained Native enslaved people through trade with or as gifts from other Natives. For example, in 1670, Jesuit colonizer Jacques Marquette received a Native enslaved man from an Odawa man. He had been captured by the Illini and traded to the Odawa.

In 1763, King Louis XV banished the Jesuits from his kingdom, including the Illinois Country. The Jesuits auctioned off their Kaskaskia property, which included slave dwellings. At this time, the Jesuits at Kaskaskia enslaved sixty-eight people. They shipped forty-eight of them down the Mississippi River by flatboat to New Orleans, where authorities under the French Crown sold them at auction.

In 1814, the Jesuits were restored. They, along with some of their enslaved people, took a flatboat from their Maryland plantations down the Ohio River to form new missions in Missouri.

The Pierre Menard house, below Fort Kaskaskia in Illinois, was built around 1802. From 1802 to 1848, enslaved people lived and labored on the property. They most likely built the house. According to slave censuses, Menard enslaved seven people in 1810, thirteen people in 1820 and twenty-two people in 1830. Researchers believe the footprints of two slave dwellings are located under two feet of post-1870s fill.

CAHOKIA, ILLINOIS

In 1698, Father Pinet and other French-Canadian priests from New France (Quebec) arrived on the bank of the Mississippi River across from a village of around four hundred Cahokia, Tamaroa and Wea to establish a mission to reach those Native people. They offered the Feast of the Immaculate Conception and mass on the banks of the river, which they named the River of Immaculate Conception.

Holy Family Parish was established in 1699 at Cahokia. Father Pinet and two workers built a cross-shaped log church and log rectory. In 1740, the church was burned. The current church, dedicated in 1799, incorporates some of the logs from the 1699 church.

There were eight or nine people enslaved by the Holy Family Parish at Cahokia in 1735. They were most likely buried in unmarked graves on the Holy Family Church grounds, along with fifty-five Revolutionary War soldiers. The enslaved probably lived in slave cabins in the park across the street from the church.

I viewed a 1787 ledger in the French language of the deaths for the Holy Family Parish that are housed at the Holy Family Museum. There are entries for enslaved people. For example, Jacques was a "negre" enslaved by Madame Beaulieu, who died at around the age of one hundred.

Nicolas Jarrot was born near Vesoul, France, in 1764, and at the age of twenty-seven, he came to the United States with a group of priests to escape the French Revolution. By 1793, after traveling through Baltimore and New Orleans, he resided in Cahokia and was a judge, attorney and captain of the territorial militia. Jarrot owned a general store and built several mills. He was also a land speculator whose total holdings may have totaled twenty-five thousand acres. He died of a fever in 1820.

The Nicolas and Julie Jarrot mansion was built by their enslaved people using hand-pressed bricks that were fired on the property from circa 1807 to 1810. The enslaved people most likely lived in log cabins behind the main house. At the time of his death in 1820, Jarrot enslaved fewer than ten people. The large stone cooking fireplace in the home's basement (removed during 1940s renovations) and the rooms on the second floor were used by the enslaved people. The second floor was not used as a living space by the Jarrot family. It was an area used for hospitality and included a guest room with a large closet, unusual for that period. On the main floor, there once was a pass-through in the wall to the right of the basement door that was used by the enslaved. It led directly to the dining room, which was part of the large central space also used as an entry hall.

Four horse skulls were found hidden inside the walls of the house. Today, three of these skulls are still in the house, and one is on display in the Cahokia Courthouse Visitor Center. It is not known why they were placed there. One possibility, which is simply speculation on my part, is that the enslaved who built the house hid them there as part of a traditional African ritual.

The Jarrots were involved in a freedom suit that led to the 1845 Illinois law outlawing slavery in the state. The French system of slavery in Illinois was created by the French Crown in 1723 and regulated by the 1724 Code Noir. The Northwest Ordinance, Illinois Constitution and various state laws created a gray area concerning the issue of slavery. The 1787 Northwest Ordinance prohibited slavery in the Illinois Territory, but at the same time, it guaranteed a resident's property rights. Since enslaved people were considered property, did the ordinance free them? The Illinois Constitution of 1818 contained an antislavery clause. Some state legislative acts said slavery was legal in Illinois. Complicating matters further was the state's system of indentured servitude, which lasted until 1865.

In 1843, Pete Jarrot, a man enslaved by Julie Jarrot, sued her for his freedom. The suit was first heard in Belleville, where the jury ruled in Julie's favor. The case moved on to the Illinois Supreme Court in 1844. A majority of the justices ruled that the Northwest Ordinance and Illinois Constitution prohibited slavery in Illinois. This ruling became law in 1845.

CONCLUSION

Our country is the world, our countrymen are all mankind.
—slogan of the Liberator *(Boston)*

I f one were able to board a time machine and travel back to early 1860s St. Louis, during the Civil War, one would find a precariously divided city under Union control that was also inhabited by many Southern sympathizers. The cityscape contained Confederate boat burners and spies, Union soldiers, civilians from both sides and free and enslaved Black people. Union army hospitals, three military prisons, James Eads's ironclad shipbuilding yard and hospital steamboats occupied the area. Fortifications, a Union horse corral, the St. Louis Arsenal and Jefferson and Benton Barracks are visible on contemporary military maps. Both Black and white refugees flooded the city as they fled from slavery or western Missouri's "Burnt District" and guerrilla warfare.

As the Civil War progressed, it became apparent that the North needed something big to turn the tide in its favor. After the Union claimed victory at Antietam, President Abraham Lincoln issued the Emancipation Proclamation (1863), freeing the enslaved people in all rebellious states. It provided the motivation necessary for the North to start winning battles and eventually end the war. The Thirteenth Amendment to the United States Constitution, which abolished slavery, was ratified on December 6, 1865, thus ending the necessity for the Underground Railroad. Unfortunately, the newly emancipated Black Americans still faced an uphill struggle during

Reconstruction and the Jim Crow era, which still continues today. Hopefully, a new Underground Railroad, one of freedom disciples and breakers of oppression, can effectively put an end to the new Jim Crow and lead us forward on the eternal path to liberty, love and peace.

> *Parting water stood and tumbled as the captives passed on through, washing off the chains of bondage: channel to a life made new.*
> —*Hymn 476, "Crashing Waters at Creation,"* Glory to God: The Presbyterian Hymnal

Note: I am constantly unearthing new information about the Underground Railroad and burial and dwelling sites of enslaved people in Missouri and Illinois. Stay tuned for volume 2.

BIBLIOGRAPHY

Books

Barringer, Floyd S., MD, and Richard L. Kuhne. *A Walk Through Oak Ridge Cemetery*. Springfield, IL: Sangamon County Historical Society, 1967. Reprint, 1997.

Basker, James G., ed. *American Antislavery Writings: Colonial Beginnings to Emancipation*. New York: Library Classics of the United States Inc., 2012.

Bradley, Marilyn. *City of Century Homes: A History of Webster Groves, Missouri*. St. Louis, MO: Marilyn Bradley, 1995.

Brown, William Wells. *Narrative of William Wells Brown, A Fugitive Slave, Written by Himself*. 1847. Chicago: e-artnow, 2020.

Burke, Henry Robert, and Charles Hart Fogle. *Washington County Underground Railroad*. Charleston, SC: Arcadia Publishing, 2004.

Caldwell, Dorothy J., ed. *Missouri Historic Sites Catalogue*. Columbia: State Historical Society of Missouri, 1963.

Carter, Chris. *Tour Essex/Kent County's Heritage Trail: Early Settlements of Africa-Canadians, Starting 1750*. Essex, ON: Tour Essex Group, 2014.

Chapman, Charles C. *Histories of Knox, Peoria, Tazewell and Fulton Counties in Illinois*. Peoria, IL: Charles C. Chapman & Co., 1878–80.

Clamorgan, Cyprian. *The Colored Aristocracy of St. Louis*. 1858. Edited with an introduction by Julie Winch. Columbia: University of Missouri Press, 1999.

Copeland, Jeffrey S. *Ain't No Harm to Kill the Devil: The Life & Legend of John Fairfield, Abolitionist for Hire*. St. Paul, MN: Paragon House, 2014.

Davison, Rosemary S. *Florissant, Missouri*. Virginia Beach, VA: Donning Co., 2002.

Delbanco, Andrew. *The War Before the War: Fugitive Slaves & the Struggle for America's Soul from the Revolution to the Civil War*. New York: Penguin Press, 2018.

Dempsey, Terrell. *Searching for Jim: Slavery in Sam Clemens' World*. Columbia: University of Missouri Press, 2003.

Deters, Ruth. *The Underground Railroad Ran Through My House! How the Intriguing Story of Dr. David Nelson's Home Uncovered a Region of Secrets*. Quincy, IL: Eleven Oaks Publishing, 2008.

Dunphy, John J. *Abolitionism & the Civil War in Southwestern Illinois*. Charleston, SC: The History Press, 2011.

———. *It Happened at the River Bend*. Alton, IL: Second Reading Publications, 2007.

Foner, Eric. *Forever Free: The Story of Emancipation & Reconstruction*. New York: Vintage Books, 2005.

Fox, Karen. *Roadside History of Western St. Louis County, Missouri*. Wildwood, MO: Wildwood Historical Society, 2019.

Frazier, Harriet C. *Runaway & Freed Missouri Slaves & Those Who Helped Them, 1763–1865*. Jefferson, NC: McFarland & Company Inc., 2004.

Goodnow, Lymon. *The History of Waukesha County, Wisconsin, Containing an Account of Its Settlement, Growth, Development, and Resources*. Chicago: Western Historical Company, 1880.

Gordon, Christopher Alan. *Fire, Pestilence & Death: St. Louis 1849*. St. Louis: Missouri Historical Society Press, 2018.

Gunther, Eileen. *In Their Own Words: Slave Life & the Power of Spirituals*. St. Louis, MO: Morning Music Publishers Inc., 2016.

Hart, Richard E. *Lincoln's Springfield: The Underground Railroad*. Springfield, IL: Sangamon County Historical Society, 2006.

Johnson, Walter. *The Broken Heart of America: St. Louis & the Violent History of the United States*. New York: Basic Books, 2020.

King, William S. *Till the Dark Angel Comes: Abolitionism & the Road to the Second American Revolution*. Yardley, PA: Westholme Publishing LLC, 2016.

Mallinckrodt, Anita M. *Freed Slaves: Ex-Slaves & Augusta Missouri's Germans During & After the Civil War*. Augusta, MO: Self-published, 1999.

———. *What They Thought (II): Missouri Immigrant, Friedrich Munch, Assesses Slavery & the Civil War, 1862*. Augusta, MO: Self-published, 1995.

McCauley Renn, Erin. *Missouri Germans & Slavery*. Hermann, MO: Deutschheim State Historic Site, n.d.

McLaurin, Milton A. *Celia, A Slave*. New York: HarperCollins, 1991.

Michna-Bales, Jeanine. *Through Darkness to Light: Photographs Along the Underground Railroad*. New York: Princeton Architectural Press, 2017.

Mobley, Jane, PhD. *Home Place: A Celebration of Life in Bridgeton, Missouri*. Bridgeton, MO: City of Bridgeton, 1993.

Morris, Ann. *Sacred Greenspace: A Survey of Cemeteries in St. Louis County*. N.p.: Self-published, 2000.

Muelder, Owen W. *The Underground Railroad in Western Illinois*. Jefferson, NC: McFarland & Company Inc., 2008.

Mutti Burke, Diane. *On Slavery's Border: Missouri's Small Slaveholding Households, 1815–1865*. Early American Places Series, 17. Athens: University of Georgia Press, 2010.

O'Bright, Alan W., and Kristen R. Marolf. *The Farm on the Gravois: Historic Structures Report*. St. Louis, MO: Ulysses S. Grant National Historic Site, 1999.

Powell, Hazel Rowena. *Adventures Underground in the Caves of Missouri*. New York: Pageant Press, 1953.

Rizzo, Dennis. *Parallel Communities: The Underground Railroad in South Jersey*. Charleston, SC: The History Press, 2008.

Rodabaugh, John. *Frenchtown*. St. Louis, MO: Sunrise, 1980.

Rother, Hubert, and Charlotte Rother. *Lost Caves of St. Louis: A History of the City's Forgotten Caves*. St. Louis, MO: Virginia Publishing, 1996.

Sappington-Concord: A History. St. Louis, MO: Sappington-Concord Historical Society, 1999.

Saunders, Delores T. *Illinois Liberty Lines: The History of the Underground Railroad*. N.p.: D.T. Saunders, 1982.

Seibert, William H. *The Underground Railroad from Slavery to Freedom: A Comprehensive History*. 1898. Mineola, NY: Dover Publications, 2006.

Still, William. *The Underground Railroad: A Selection of Authorized Narratives, Abridged*. 1872. London: Arcturus Publishing Ltd., 2017.

Swinger, Patricia. *The Story of Jacob Zumwalt & His Fort*. O'Fallon, MO: O'Fallon Community Foundation, 2018.

Theissing, Andrew J., ed. *In the Walnut Grove: A Consideration of the People Enslaved In & Around Florissant, Missouri*. Florissant, MO: Florissant Valley Historical Society, 2020.

Tobin, Jaqueline, and Raymond G. Dobard, PhD. *Hidden in Plain View: A Secret Story of Quilts & the Underground Railroad*. New York: Anchor Books, 1999.

Turner, Glennette Tilley. *The Underground Railroad in DuPage County, Illinois*. Toronto, ON: Williams-Wallace Publishers Inc., 1986.

Van Horne-Lane, Janice. *Safe Houses & the Underground Railroad in East Central, Ohio*. Charleston, SC: The History Press, 2010.

Von Gruben, Jill F. *Early Churches of Meramec Township, St. Louis County, Missouri*. Wildwood, MO: Wildwood Historical Society, 2018.

Wright, John A., Sr. *African Americans in Downtown St. Louis*. Charleston, SC: Arcadia Publishing, 2003.

———. *Discovering African American St. Louis: A Guide to Historic Sites*. 2nd ed. St. Louis, MO: Missouri Historical Society Press, 2002.

———. *Missouri Slave Narratives: A Folk History of Slavery in Missouri from Interviews with Former Slaves, Typewritten Records Prepared by the Federal Writer's Project, 1936–1938*. Bedford, MA: Applewood Books, n.p. Washington, D.C.: Library of Congress, n.d.

Articles, Brochures and Booklets

African-American Historic Sites of Independence. Independence, MO: Independence, Missouri Tourism Division, n.d.

Chesnutt, Florence. *Cooper County Church Sketches.* Pilot Grove, MO: Cooper County Historical Society, 1993.

———. *Old Pleasant Green Underground.* Reprint, Pilot Grove, MO: Cooper County Historical Society, 2008.

Father Dickson Cemetery: Walking Tour & Map. Rev. ed., St. Louis, MO: Friends of Father Dickson Cemetery, 2014.

Fox, Karen. "Elijah Madison: The Courage & Perseverance of One Man." *Magazine of the Missouri Historical Society* 38, no. 1 (Spring 2018): 18–29.

French Creole Corridor: Mid-Mississippi River Valley. 3rd ed. St. Louis, MO: Les Amis, 2013.

Historically Awesome St. Charles. St. Charles, MO: Historic St. Charles, n.d.

The Kimmswick Historical Society Walking Tour Guide. Kimmswick, MO: Kimmswick Historical Society, n.d.

National Register of Historic Places Inventory nomination form: Des Peres Presbyterian Church. Prepared by Noelle Soren. Missouri Office of Historic Preservation, Jefferson City, MO, 1977.

Orr, Corey. "The Raid on Danville, Missouri, October 14, 1864." *Guardian* 11, no. 2 (Summer 2020): n.p.

———. "A Slave a Soldier." *Guardian* 10, no. 3 (Fall 2019): n.p.

Pinsker, Matthew. "Slave Stampedes on the Missouri Borderlands." 2020. www.housedivided.dickenson.edu.

Racine County, Wisconsin Roots of Freedom Underground Railroad Heritage Trail: A Self-Guided Walking/Driving Tour Across Some of the Nation's Most Hallowed Ground. Racine, WI: Racine County Roots of Freedom Underground Railroad Heritage Trail, 2008.

Ripley County, Indiana Underground Railroad: Five Driving Trails. Versailles, IN: Ripley County Tourism Bureau, n.d.

See Quincy. "Historic Quincy, Illinois: Gateway City, 1835–1865: A Self-Guided Driving Tour of the Historic City on the Bay." www.seequincy.com.

Slavery: Cause & Catalyst of the Civil War. Washington, D.C.: National Park Service, United States Department of the Interior, n.d.

Southeastern Indiana Trails to Freedom: Underground Railroad Driving Tours. Indianapolis: Indiana Underground Railroad Coalition, in cooperation with the Indiana Office of Tourism Development through the lieutenant governor's Quality of Place Initiative, n.d.

"Survey of the Coleman Slave Cemetery (23SL2333) in Wildwood, St. Louis County, Missouri." Prepared for City of Wildwood by the Archaeological Research Center of St. Louis Inc., St. Louis, MO, 2013.

Thornbury, Lee A. *The Kelton House Museum & Garden*. Columbus, OH: Bergman Books, 2001.

The Underground Railroad in Erie County, Ohio. Sandusky, OH: Ohio's Lake Erie Shores and Island, n.d.

Underground Railroad: Official National Park Handbook. Washington, D.C.: National Park Service, United States Department of the Interior, n.d.

Upper Alton Home & House Tour, Sunday, May 18, 1997. Alton, IL: Alton Museum of History and Art, 1997.

Williams, Scott K. "Slavery in St. Louis." 2016. www.usgennet.org/usa/mo/county/stlouis/slavery.htm.

Your Guide to the History & Sites of the Underground Railroad in Jacksonville, Illinois & Morgan County. Jacksonville, IL: Jacksonville Area Convention and Visitor's Bureau, n.d.

ABOUT THE AUTHOR

Julie Nicolai is a local St. Louis historian and has been studying the Underground Railroad in Missouri, Illinois and Kansas for twenty-five years. She has bachelor's and master's degrees in art history and archaeology from Washington University in St. Louis and has written articles for the Missouri Historical Society, the New York Silver Society and the Morse-Libby Mansion. She is currently working on a book about Jaccard silver in a local museum's collections. She lives in St. Louis and loves to travel anywhere to experience the Underground Railroad.